THE TIMES TRAVEL LIBRARY

Times Editions, 422 Thomson Road, Singapore 1129
© Copyright by Times Editions, 1986

Printed by Tien Wah Press, Singapore
Colour separation by Columbia, Singapore
Typeset by Type Graphic, Singapore

Cover: The Dayabumi Complex, designed in the shape
of an Islamic star, is illuminated Thursday nights for
Friday mosque days. The 36-storey government
showcase was designed by Malaysian architects
incorporating Arabic and Moorish styles.
Endpapers: This traditional wood carving, nearly a
century-old, was designed after a common wild fern and
was once used as a door panel for ventilation. It is at
the National Museum.
Frontispiece: The K.L. High Court building, on the
Gombak River, is decorated for the King's coronation.

ISBN: 9971-40-029-4

KUALA LUMPUR

Text and Photographs by Marlane Guelden

Designed by Leonard Lueras

First Edition 1986

TIMES EDITIONS

"Be it known to all men that by these presents,
that We with the assent of His Royal Highness
Sultan Salahuddin Abdul Aziz Shah ibni al-
marhum Sultan Hisamuddin Alam Shah Al-Haj,
Sultan and Ruler of Selangor and all its pos-
sessions, and with the bountiful and special assent
are pleased to Bestow, Embody, Declare and
Promise that said Municipality of Kuala Lumpur
shall as from 1st. Feb. 1972, and for all time shall
be a city and shall be called and named the City of
Kuala Lumpur in place of the Municipality of the
Federal Capital of Kuala Lumpur and from then
and always have all rights, freedom, privileges and
immunity befitting a city."

Given at Our Istana Negara in Our capital at Kuala
Lumpur on the 1st day of Feb. 1972.

—By order of His Majesty Yang di-Pertuan Agong.
Signed: Tun Abdul Razak bin Dato Hussein.

This page: The Islamic Centre Complex, the country's first centre for the study and administration of Islam, is designed after a typical Middle East castle with a walled courtyard to hold 6,000 people.

***Following pages:** Muslims listen to talks by the King and other leaders during Prophet Mohammad's birthday at the National Mosque; The Kau Ong Yah temple in Kampung Ampang is thronged with devotees after a firewalking ceremony during the Nine Emperor Gods festival; and Hindu believers give offerings to the priests at Batu Caves during Thaipusam.*

Contents

Affectionately Yours
page 15

Historical Chronology
page 26

The Majestic
page 37

Lat's Lot
page 38

On Becoming Malaysian
page 40

Malaysia's Ghostbusters
page 53

Magic Daggers
page 66

Maps
page 70

K.L. Trivia
page 72

K.L. Tours
page 74

Off the Beaten Track
page 79

K.L. Best Bets
page 82

Travel Notes
page 86

Index
page 92

Kuala Lumpur

Affectionately Yours

At the tip of the land mass that points down from Thailand and Burma is the Malay Peninsula — romantically referred to by poet John Milton in *Paradise Lost* as the Golden Chersonese. In 1881 it had only three-quarters of a million inhabitants — less than half Malays — and was described by one travel writer as having no ancient history, great wars, valuable literature or impressive ruins that attract world attention.

Instead the Malay Peninsula, by a quirk of geography, was an important crossroads between the great civilizations of China and India. From India in particular, Malaya liberally borrowed religion, art, literature, and customs. The jutting peninsula, open to the Straits of Malacca on one side and the South China Sea on the other, was in the heart of the spice, silk, and porcelain trade in the 15th century. Merchants waited out the monsoons here before continuing their journeys. Chinese came with their junks during the northeast monsoon and Arab and Indian traders arrived with the southwest winds.

And 400 years later, the peninsula's natural resources would draw more traders, world powers, and labourers to reap the benefits of this fertile land — soon to be the world's largest producer of tin, rubber and palm oil. In the heart of this country — now called Malaysia — is a young city with the decidedly unromantic name of Muddy River Mouth.

Today Kuala Lumpur is a city in a hurry to transform itself from a sleepy town to a major, modern world capital as quickly as possible. Sleek narrow skyscrapers cloaked in opaque black and silvery mirrored walls or white curved neo-Islamic concrete seem to erupt overnight from the ground.

Trees inserted in the middle of sidewalks appear almost as an afterthought. Six-lane highways pulsate day and night with cars, an astonishing number of them Mercedes Benzes, BMWs and Volvos. It often seems there is scarcely a car in the city more than four years old. Trishaws have virtually disappeared. In the remaining few, wizened operators pedal ageing passengers with groceries.

Dodging between the cars with frightening adeptness are motorcycles, which nearly outnumber cars. Their cowboy-like riders appear oblivious to the laws of physics. The white line is their highway as they squeeze between cars. At traffic lights, the motorcyclists weave to the front, using their hands to snake between car bumpers and fenders. They wear rubber thongs and their bare, unprotected feet make

them appear vulnerable. Motorcycle helmets are required by law for all but Sikhs wearing pastel-coloured sacred turbans and Muslims with white head scarves, or *serbans*, often proof of a pilgrimage to Mecca.

Weathered men, looking like World War II aviators, wear antique crash helmets with leather ear flaps sometimes held on with plastic string. Children are pressed so closely between parents that only their spindly legs protrude on both sides. Visors, prohibited for fear they could be used as masks by robbers, are replaced by bandanas covering mouths — giving the impression of Wild West holdup men. Others wear jackets backwards with

Three views of Kuala Lumpur. The city at night (preceding pages) is framed by surrounding hills. The junction of the Klang and Gombak rivers (left) is still a commercial hub. Super highways, or lebuhraya (above), ease congested traffic.

15

collars up to cut the wind and rain, a look so common it has become almost fashionable.

That is the Kuala Lumpur the visitor sees when stepping out of a modern downtown hotel. But there is something deeper. A powerful dragon is said to lie under the Golden Triangle, an imaginary area that encompasses the city's financial and hotel districts. At one end of the triangle sits the pride of the government, a new 38-storey office building, the

small red altar to appease the deity they believe is the Malay god of the land. In a dilapidated shanty, a respected Malay medicine man, a *bomoh*, helps an Indian woman find her wandering husband using verses from the Koran. He warns visitors against stepping over a powerful plant that causes abortions. It is this deeper, less obvious dimension which makes Kuala Lumpur a fascinating and alluring metropolis to explore.

Bangunan Tabung Haji, shaped like a nuclear powerplant's cooling tower. Profits from rents will be used to fund trips for the poor to Mecca.

According to widespread stories in the Kuala Lumpur business community, another new skyscraper in the triangle was originally designed with a sloping roof. But a Chinese geomancer who was called in advised that the sloping roof would bring bad luck, since the building is owned by a finance company. The money, he said, would slide off. Reportedly the building's roof was flattened and presumably the money remains in place.

At each construction site, Chinese workers offer incense and fruit — but no pork — to a

Masjid (mosque) Jame, built in 1909 on the site of first Malay cemetery, was the main Friday mosque until 1967 when the National Mosque was built. It is a replica of a north Indian mosque. The altar, or kiblat, *faces Mecca.*

Only about 130 years ago, Kuala Lumpur was a bit of jungle land with a few *attap* huts between the Klang and Gombak rivers, the muddy river mouth the city is named after. When 87 Chinese miners poled boats up the Klang River laden with rice, opium, muskets and spears, they could go no farther when they reached the shallow waters at this divide. With the help of a Malay medicine man armed with a divining rod, they found the valuable commodity they were looking for — tin. These early Chinese miners paid a high price for their adventure. Most died of malaria within the first month. But more coolies took their place. With wooden yokes across their backs and wearing pointed wicker hats, they climbed down into deep pits, loaded dirt into baskets and carried it to the surface where the precious metal was extracted. Within two years tin was being exported. Malaysia's capital city was born.

The city lies in a fertile basin buttressed on the east by the mountainous main range that runs all the way to Thailand. The Malay Peninsula has been described as resembling the head of an anteater eating an ant — Singapore is the ant. Kuala Lumpur is located near the animal's mouth, in the state of Selangor. The peninsula has a population of about 13 million, less than one-tenth that of neighbouring Indonesia. And the states of Sabah and Sarawak

independent and wealthy state with such promising tin deposits that both the British and the Dutch had tried to gain a monopoly over it. By the time the sultan died 31 years later, the lure of tin had set the stage for a civil war.

The sultan depended largely on his chiefs to control the river settlements. They in turn collected taxes on goods travelling by the state's five rivers and lived in reasonable harmony. But as tin mining developed, Chinese

on the nearby island of Borneo contribute another 2.7 million to the country's population — making a total of almost 16 million.

In the 18th century the coastal state of Selangor, north of Malacca, was founded and ruled by the Bugis from the southern Celebes in what is now Indonesia. A few thousand Sumatran Malays lived inland. The Bugis, fierce warriors who fought in chain mail suits, were known as mercenaries, pirates, clever traders and good sailors.

The Bugis established the first sultanate of Selangor and used the state as one of their bases for a dynasty that controlled much of the Malay Peninsula until the Dutch defeated them in the 1780s. The British superseded the Dutch but left the Bugis alone in their less populated inland wilderness.

When the Bugis Sultan Muhammad inherited Selangor in 1826, the region was an

merchants from the Straits Settlements, comprised of Penang, Malacca and Singapore, pressed for concessions in tin-rich areas. Suddenly land became a valuable commodity.

Sultan Muhammad had unsuccessfully tried to mine up Selangor's Klang River. He borrowed heavily from Chinese *towkays,* or businessmen, in Malacca but lost it all. Recklessly passing through Malacca one day, he was stopped by merchants demanding repayment of their money. Two brother princes paid the debt. Sultan Muhammad arranged for one, Raja Abdullah, to marry his niece and made him chief of the Klang River area in 1854. This angered Raja Mahdi, the son of the former

Early 20th century shophouses line Jalan Tuanku Abdul Rahman, named after Malaysia's first king. This was a major shopping district from the 1940s–1960s before modern shopping complexes were built elsewhere.

Klang chief, who expected to inherit the area and its lucrative tin income.

Raja Abdullah, an experienced miner, succeeded where Sultan Muhammad failed. He sent the 87 miners up the Klang River looking for tin, which they discovered in abundance in the Ampang area of Kuala Lumpur. Some historians say Raja Abdullah must thus be considered the founder of Kuala Lumpur, although most assign that role to an enterprising Chinese named Yap Ah Loy.

The demand for tin was high, because of the development of the canning process in the West, and coolies were needed to mine it. Coolies who could not pay their own passage from China were given room to squat on a boat and were promptly sold for a few dollars to employers on arrival in Penang, Malacca or Singapore. The mine owner usually had the alcohol, opium, and gambling concessions and workers often were in debt to the company store for years. They came expecting to stay only long enough to earn their fortunes and return to China, but for thousands Malaya would become their permanent home.

Malay chiefs preferred to collect tin taxes from one Chinese leader in an area, called the Capitan China, pronounced cheena. In Kuala Lumpur, Yap Ah Loy held that position from 1868 until his death in 1885. At the age of 17 he was recruited from his Hakka community in Guangdong province, China. He worked his way up from pig seller and bodyguard to mine manager. He also earned a reputation as a good fighter and was appointed Capitan China of a mining area controlled by his society. He was given the same position in Kuala Lumpur at the early age of 31 — the town's third and most powerful Capitan China.

Yap Ah Loy soon had to face the seven-year Selangor Civil War, a struggle among Malay chiefs for control of the tin revenues. The war came very close to killing both him and his burgeoning mining town. The war began in 1866 when Raja Mahdi drove Raja Abdullah's forces out of Klang to claim it for himself.

As the civil war spread inland to the tin mines, Yap Ah Loy took the side of Raja Abdullah. The battle intensified in Kuala Lumpur where two groups of rival Chinese miners — both Hakkas — took opposing sides in the conflict.

Street hawkers, a common sight in K.L., wheel their bicycle carts into Petaling Street for the night market after a late afternoon rain storm. During the day, the same fruit carts crowd the street until the police force them onto the sidewalks

Yap Ah Loy paid $50 in silver for every enemy head delivered to his home in market square. Business was good. The bodies of fighters and horses lay in piles around the town. Later, a British resident reported finding 16 skeletons buried under the foundation of one house. Two skeletons were embracing.

A Dutch mercenary officer named Van Hagen led Yap Ah Loy's forces in a last-ditch stand to save the city at Bukit Nanas, Pine-apple Hill. Van Hagen finally had to give up the fort and tried to escape through the jungle but his guides led the party into the enemy camp — and death. Yap Ah Loy escaped by another route but reportedly came upon the bodies of 1,700 of his men. When Yap Ah Loy finally emerged from the jungle to rejoin his allies, he was wearing only underwear. It was 1872 and Kuala Lumpur had fallen to Mahdi's faction after battles involving 4000 men.

With the support of the British governor of Singapore, more soldiers were brought in from another state and Mahdi was defeated once and for all. The war was finally over. Yap Ah Loy returned to a devastated Kuala Lumpur where he talked the miners into staying in the "bad luck" town and established credit in Singapore and Malacca to get the mines functioning. But prices on the tin market dropped to a 30-year low. When all seemed lost, the tin price jumped and the city flour-ished. Yap Ah Loy became the largest tin miner and owner of more than half of the town. It was called miner's luck.

After the war, he was officially installed as

The roti *man (above) drives through neighbour-hoods and city streets honking his horn for bread, tapioca chips, and cakes. The neatly arranged* Mamak *shop (right) clings to a building wall. Such shops are often run by Indian Muslims.*

The National Dance Company, *performing for the King's coronation, choreographs a contemporary dance based on traditional movement. It is a morality play about a man who sells his soul, and his mother's corpse, to the devil but is later cured by a medicine man and brought back to Allah by an* imam.

OLD MARKET
K. LUMPUR

Old Market Square in 1925 was the heart of town. The Hongkong and Shanghai
Banking Corp. building, centre, was an impressive three-storey structure. Today
this is still a busy square with several shophouses still standing.

Historical Chronology

1766 — Bugis nobleman Raja Lumu is installed as the first sultan of Selangor and given the title Sultan Sallehuddin. According to Malay custom he has the right to rule because his appointment is made by Perak royalty who claim descent from the 15th century Malacca sultanate.

1857 — Raja Abdullah finances a successful tin mining expedition up the Klang River. Eighty-seven miners land at the confluence of the Klang and Gombak rivers and go to Ampang where they find tin.

1868 — A resourceful Hakka Chinese immigrant, Yap Ah Loy, is appointed the third Capitan China of Kuala Lumpur. Yap institutes harsh punishments for stealing — first offence, the thief is dragged through town; second offence, his ear is cut off; and third offence, his throat is cut. Theft drops.

1866–73 — The Selangor Civil War, fought among Malay royalty for control of the tin mines, leaves Kuala Lumpur in shambles.

1874 — Without any clear directive from London, colonial Governor Sir Andrew Clarke reverses Britain's non-intervention policy. He forces Selangor Sultan Abdul Samad to accept a British resident to advise the state's viceroy, Tunku Kudin. Clarke uses a piracy incident involving the sultan's men as a way to obtain the agreement.

1875 — James Guthrie Davidson, a businessman who had backed the winning side of the civil war, is appointed the first British resident of Selangor.

1878 — The world price of tin doubles and saves Kuala Lumpur from financial disaster.

1880 — The new resident, Captain Bloomfield Douglas, moves the state capital from Klang to Kuala Lumpur. But he has such an enmity for the Chinese, he

puts the government offices on the west side of the Klang River away from Yap Ah Loy's town.

1881 — A fire destroys most of the town at the beginning of the year and at the end of the year a major flood leaves miners unable to pay their debts before the Chinese New Year as is Chinese custom.

1882 — Frank Swettenham is appointed resident. Streets are widened and the town rebuilt with tile and brick. Within five years there will be 518 brick buildings in Kuala Lumpur. When the town is planned, the government reserves Petaling Street for brothels. It is accepted that brothels are a necessary evil with one woman to every 10 men. European men regularly visit Japanese brothels in Petaling Street during the early 1900s. It is estimated in 1923 that from 25 to 80 per cent of European men have or have had veneral disease. Brothels in the city are finally outlawed 50 years

later in 1931.

1883 — Malaya becomes the world's largest tin producer, surpassing Britain, which held the position for more than 600 years.

1886 — A railway line is built between Klang and Kuala Lumpur and an old engine renamed the Lady Clarke chugs in at about 50 kmph to cheering crowds. Sultan Abdul Samad, 81, says it is the best bullock cart he has ever ridden in.

1888 — Alfred Venning, a planter from Ceylon, proposes to turn a swampy ravine outside town into a botanical garden. It takes him 10 years, but finally the 70-hectare Lake Gardens is completed.

1890 — A town council, inappropriately called the Sanitary Board, is created to advise the resident on running the capital. The board, with representatives from different ethnic groups, passes pragmatic laws such as outlawing the pouring of kerosene on a rat and setting it on fire. This not uncommon practice was deemed "cruelty to a rat".

1894 — The foundation stone of the State Secretariat is laid. A plan to build in Renaissance style is dropped for a more apt Islamic style. Australia in 1982 donates money to re-copper the black painted domes.

1896 — The Federated Malay States — Perak, Pahang, Negri Sembilan and Selangor — are formed and Kuala Lumpur is named the capital, partly because of its central location. All administrative functions move to the city.

1897 — The coffee market collapses and frantic coffee planters turn to rubber just as the automobile industry is increasing the demand for rubber tyres. By 1905 rubber is booming. The Singapore agency houses of Harrisons & Crosfield and Guthrie & Co., and rubber manufacturers including Dunlop establish offices in Kuala Lumpur. By 1920 Malaya will produce over half of the world's rubber.

1909 — A Federal Council, comprised of residents and sultans, is formed in Kuala Lumpur to rule the four states. From this council the legislative council and later the country's parliament will evolve.

1910 — Doctors at Kuala Lumpur's Institute of Medical Research make a breakthrough on beri-beri, the deadly disease caused by a vitamin B deficiency that has killed many Chinese miners who ate polished rice. From 1890–1900 the Kuala Lumpur hospital treats 16,000 people for beri-beri and 3,000 of them die. The opium tax farm is also abolished and the government produces and sells opium to guarantee the quality. Opium provides one of the largest sources of government income until the 1920s. Opium is not banned until after World War II.

1912 — Chinese riot. Chinese miners cut off the long pigtails of rickshaw drivers, symbolizing the demise of the Manchu Dynasty. And a battle lasting a week breaks out among clans and spreads from Petaling

Yap Ah Loy, Capitan China of Kuala Lumpur from 1868–1885, saw his mining town nearly destroyed by civil war, fire, flood, and financial disaster. He is considered to be the founder of modern Kuala Lumpur.

Street to an Ampang mine. The local militia ends the so-called "Tauchang Riots". A Chinese Advisory Board is proposed to make the British aware of problems in the Chinese community.

1918 — The first tin dredge is installed in Selangor. Within 12 years, more than 100 are brought into the country. Chinese mining companies cannot afford the $10 million cost of installing a dredge so by 1937 European investors are producing two-thirds of the country's tin.

1919 — Mass violent demonstrations are held in Kuala Lumpur by Chinese to protest Japan receiving Chinese territory under the Versailles Treaty. Concerned that political activities are rampant among students, the colonial government cracks down on Chinese schools.

1920 — The annual death rate from malaria in Kuala Lumpur is cut in half by the creation of covered drains. After the discovery in India in 1900 that malaria is transmitted by mosquitoes, the Kuala Lumpur officials are the first to put the knowledge to work by draining swamps around Klang.

1926 — Central Kuala Lumpur is flooded in a metre of water. Post office workers arrive in sampans and

enter through windows while rickshaw pullers form teams of five to pull riders through the water. The Chartered Bank is flooded and millions of dollars in wet bills are laid on the *padang* to dry, watched by an armed guard. A straight channel with high walls is built for the Klang River and floods become less frequent.

1941 — On December 8, the Japanese launch simultaneous attacks on Pearl Harbor, the Phillippines, Hong Kong and Malaya. On January 11, they overrun Kuala Lumpur. In 70 days they control the whole Malay Peninsula including Singapore. They recognize the power of the Malay sultans and guarantee their authority in religious matters.

1945 — The Japanese surrender and the communist Malayan People's Anti-Japanese Army (MPAJA) comes out of the jungle, disarms the Japanese, and claims credit for the victory. For several weeks before the British return, the communists terrorize the public.

1946 — In an effort to unify the country and give the Chinese and Indians equal status with Malays, the British convince the sultans to endorse the Malayan Union which gives all races equal citizenship rights, takes away almost all the sultans' powers, and creates a central law making body. The Malays feel their rights as the indigenous people are usurped for the first time and object strongly. They unite under The United Malays National Organization (UMNO).

1948 — Backed by UMNO, the Federation of Malaya is created as an alternative to the Malayan Union. It gives power to the sultans, safeguards the special position of Malays and gives restricted citizen rights to non-Malays. Singapore is a separate colony.

1948–1960 — The "Emergency" is declared when the Malayan Communist Party begins an insurrection by instigating strikes, forming a guerrilla army and killing planters. During the 12-year guerrilla war nearly 10,000 civilians, troops and police are killed before the communists are controlled.

1952 — The British permit the first municipal elections to encourage Malayan self-reliance. UMNO and the Malayan Chinese Association (MCA) form a temporary partnership under the banner of the Alliance Party and win their first victory.

1955 — Federal elections are held for the first time. The Malayan Indian Congress (MIC) joins the Alliance and the new coalition wins in a landslide. The Alliance, later called the National Front coalition, will become the country's ruling political coalition.

1957 — Independence — or Merdeka — is granted. It is agreed that a king will be elected by the nine sultans every five years as a constitutional monarch. The sultans are given authority over religious matters. A two-house parliament is formed and Tunku Abdul Rahman is chosen the first prime minister. English and Malay are the official languages.

1963 — The new country of Malaysia, comprised of

British officials, standing nearly waist deep in water in front of downtown K.L. government buildings, survey the damage from a major flood of the Klang and Gombak rivers about 1926.

Malaya, Singapore, Sarawak, and Sabah, is formed with Kuala Lumpur as the capital.

1963–1966 — In a battle termed the "Confrontation," Indonesia invades the east Malaysian states of Sabah and Sarawak and parts of the peninsula, claiming the residents of these territories were not consulted about joining Malaysia. At the same time, the Philippines lay claim to North Borneo (Sabah). Indonesia signs a peace agreement in 1966 after a change in administration and hostilities cease.

1965 — Tunku Abdul Rahman expels Singapore from the newly formed country after Singapore refuses to give Malays special privileges and attempts to gain power over the more conservative Malaysian Chinese Association. Singapore protests.

1969 — An emotionally charged general election results in major losses by the Alliance and the opposition parties celebrate. Malays, fearful of losing control of their country, are angered. On May 13 racial riots in Kuala Lumpur kill anywhere from 200 to 800 people. The government declares a state of emergency, dissolves parliament and suspends the constitution. Tun Abdul Razak takes over as prime minister.

1971 — The New Economic Policy is passed to attempt to fight poverty and give Malays a larger share of the economic pie. The plan calls for Malays owning one-third of the corporate wealth by 1990. In 1969, Malays own only 1 ½ per cent of assets of limited companies.

1971 — Kuala Lumpur floods again. Nine people die, 795 houses are destroyed, and 30,000 people are evacuated. Flooding persists into the 1980s.

1972 — The king officially makes Kuala Lumpur a city.

1974 — Kuala Lumpur becomes a federal territory, separate from the state of Selangor.

1983 — The Heritage of Malaysia Trust is formed to preserve historical buildings.

1984 — The Majestic Hotel, historically a meeting place for planters and political parties, is converted into the National Art Gallery.

1985 — The 1936 Art Deco style Central Market, dubbed the city's largest room, is temporarily saved from destruction and converted into a cultural centre. Merchants move to three new markets.

1985 — Malaysia produces its own car, the Proton Saga, named after a hard red seed. It is built in joint venture with Mitsubishi Motor Corp. of Japan.

Capitan China with all the rights of a Malay chief. He kept the peace, built a primitive hospital, constructed roads, collected taxes and acted as magistrate in mining disputes. He is commonly acknowledged as the true founder of the city of Kuala Lumpur.

The British had an official non-intervention policy for the Malay Peninsula. They wanted to make profits from the area but not to interfere in local politics that might lead to costly wars.

become the undisputed trading center and the capital was moved.

To save money Douglas moved buildings up from Klang and built government offices on the west side of the Klang River, leaving the disreputable east bank to Yap Ah Loy. At the time there were 220 houses in Kuala Lumpur, 70 of which were in the Malay section. Prostitutes outnumbered homes and 12 opium stores were open for business. Yap Ah Loy's

The policy, however, was regularly broken when investments were threatened. Chinese and European companies with tin mining concessions in Selangor urged the British to safeguard their properties during the civil war. A piracy incident gave the British an excuse to press Selangor Sultan Abdul Samad to accept a British adviser in 1874.

James Guthrie Davidson, who had helped finance the winning side in the civil war, became the first British resident in Selangor's capital, Klang. He was succeeded by Captain Bloomfield Douglas, who resisted moving the government upriver to Kuala Lumpur. But four years later, in 1880, Kuala Lumpur had

__The 1911 Railway Station__ is believed to have been originally designed for a Moscow trade fair and later built in K.L. with snow gutters and a roof to withstand about two metres of snow. It was completely gutted in 1986 to modernize the interior.

impressive house was at the base of the market area, next to a rickety shed housing the market and a popular gambling hall — both owned by Yap Ah Loy. The whole southern end of town, now Hang Kasturi, Bandar and Petaling streets, was filled with the Capitan China's various businesses — cattle and smelting sheds, pig stys, tapioca mills, and slaughter houses. In 1885, Yap Ah Loy died of complications arising from bronchitis at the age of 48. With the expansion of British rule, the position of Capitan China was eventually dropped.

Disaster struck Kuala Lumpur in 1881. A fire, started in an opium shop, burnt most of the town and a flood destroyed many mines. But Frank Swettenham, who replaced Douglas as resident, was an enthusiastic 32-year-old with a persuasive personality, the knack for compromise and the energy to rebuild. Over the next 22 years Swettenham would become the first Resident-General and later the High Commissioner of the Federated Malay States. He ordered the town rebuilt and the construction of a rail line to Klang, later extended to Singapore and Penang. Kuala Lumpur's palace-like 1911 railway station is a monument to the importance of the railway line.

Swettenham saw another advancement come to Malaya — rubber. At first Swettenham had ridiculed H.N. "Mad" Ridley, head of the Singapore Botanical Gardens, an outspoken advocate of rubber. Ridley had developed a way to tap trees continually without harm. Originally grown only experimentally or to shade the lucrative coffee plantations, rubber soared when prices were spurred by the popularity of the automobile and the need for pneumatic tyres. Thousands of Tamil workers from southern India were imported to work the plantations. By 1920 Malaya was producing 53 per cent of the world's rubber.

Under the British residential system, the residents gave advice and expected it to be followed, but naturally much depended on the good relationship between the Resident and the sultan. In exchange, the sultans and chiefs earned a hefty income from taxes, received British protection and limited their decisions to religious matters. Gradually the British consolidated their power and soon ruled four states — Selangor, Perak, Negri Sembilan and Pahang. The sultans eventually agreed to a British proposal to unify the four states into the Federated Malay States with one central Resident-General. The power of the rulers was further reduced and all government functions were centralized in Kuala Lumpur, the administrative capital, in 1896.

A tax on opium was a major source of British income until the 1920s, providing one-tenth of the revenue from the federated states in the early 1900s. Wealthy and respected mine owners controlled much of the import and conversion of the drug. They said miners would riot if not given opium. It was not banned until after World War II.

For the small European community, the turn of the century was an era of formal dress, cricket and clubs. New arrivals in town would leave calling cards in little boxes outside fashionable colonial homes and wait to be invited to tea. One could buy pate de foie gras, crab, pigeon, three types of champagne and other imported European delicacies.

The Selangor Club was the first popular gathering spot. The club's nickname, the Spotted Dog, has several possible origins. One story tells of how the police commissioner's

wife used to tie her two dalmations outside the club while she went inside to sip gin slings. But other historians say the nickname came from a derogatory reference to the club's practice of allowing a few select Asians as members.

The Lake Club, with a higher membership fee, was founded in 1890 for those who preferred an all-European club. It is located in the Lake Gardens, a 70-hectare park on the outskirts of town designed by a forward-thinking

treasurer of the state.

Many British also believed that the heat and humidity of the tropics was physically and mentally debilitating. After four years, men became lethargic, nervous, forgetful and sometimes suicidal. Home leave was given only every six years. The next best thing to returning to the cool climate of England was to retreat to a hill station, similar to those built in India. Several were established around Kuala Lumpur, most notably Fraser's Hill and Cameron Highlands. They serve the same purpose for city dwellers today.

The British in 1899 set aside 90 hectares for an agricultural settlement to bring Malay

Children at the Sungai Buloh leprosarium (above) play in a hospital corridor. Cameron Highlands (following pages), a popular retreat for city residents, is carpeted with tea plantations that look like soft rugs from a distance.

farmers closer to town. In exchange for free land, Malays were required to farm and learn traditional crafts, such as weaving and wood carving. The plan failed miserably when most of the poor residents opted to work in the town. The reserve is now called Kampung Baru — new village — and provides one of the few remaining examples of traditional Malay *kampung* housing in Kuala Lumpur.

The British ruled Malaya until their crush-

but their role as protector was over. Malayans agitated for independence and in 1957 the Union Jack was lowered for the last time on the *padang*, the large open field in the city centre.

Today one can still see the remnants of 77 years of British rule. Malaysian law is based on English common law. Judges wear white curled wigs and long black robes and higher court proceedings are in English, a practice regularly discussed with irritation in Malaysia's Parlia-

ing defeat by the Japanese in 1942 when the Malay Peninsula and Singapore were overrun in little over two months. The Japanese required government workers to bow to the Imperial Palace and exercise before work, but wages were so meagre many became involved in the black market. Domestic animals were eaten. Trees and bushes were destroyed bringing flies, mosquitoes and malaria. There was little physical damage to the city, until the Allies, while preparing to invade, bombed the railway workshops and destroyed part of the city's museum. The Japanese surrendered in September 1945.

The British would return after World War II

Malaysian school boys (above) compete for a rugby trophy on the Selangor Club padang. Clerks at the K.L. Stock Exchange (right) write share prices for those shouting orders to buy and sell tin, oil palm, rubber and other stocks.

ment. Some Malaysians speak in clipped British accents that startle the visitor. Cricket still survives and matches are regularly played on the *padang* in front of the Selangor Club. Some of the buildings that symbolize Kuala Lumpur — the secretariat, railway station and old mosque — were designed by British architects under colonial rule.

Nevertheless, the city's recent colonial past seems to have left little lasting impression. Enduring cultural traditions like Chinese ancestor worship, the Indian caste system and Malay *bomohs* are far more influential.

To put a Malay stamp on this historically Chinese town, the pointed Minangkabau roofs and tiered *kampung*-styled roofs have been grafted onto modern high-rises. Street names have been changed to give credit to Malay royalty rather than British administrators. Birch Street, named after a resident assas-

The Majestic

The Majestic Hotel — Kuala Lumpur's last major historic colonial hostelry — has been compared to the Oriental in Bangkok and the Raffles in Singapore. In its heyday, it was a gathering place for the colonial elite and before independence it witnessed the political struggles that created Malaysia. But by the 1980s it catered to low-budget tourists who didn't mind the red vinyl chairs and imitation-wood formica tables.

It was nearly destroyed in 1977, when the owners made plans to replace it with a 22-storey high-rise. But it was saved eventually when the government designated it an historic building and bought it under compulsory acquisition in 1983. The ultimate solution for its salvation lay in converting it into a National Art Gallery — although not without a loud public outcry.

At the time the decision seemed to please no one. Preservationists mourned the loss of the hotel that had witnessed half a century of the country's history, while artists were skeptical about using small bedrooms to house artworks and preferred a new art gallery.

But today both sides seem to be pleased, although problems persist. The artists are glad to finally have a sizable home while the preservationists are relieved the building was saved with few changes.

"Well done, well done, chaps," commented an interior designer who helped collect 4,000 signatures in an 11th hour attempt to save the hotel. She and other young professionals who gathered for the fight stayed on to form the Friends of the Heritage of Malaysia Society, to help publicise the plight of other old buildings.

Sitting on a hill overlooking the Moorish railway station, the Majestic still conveys some of its old grandeur with a curved driveway, covered entrance, mock-Roman columns and detailed cornices. Designed by a Dutch architect and built in 1932 with 51 rooms, it was the first of the "big" hotels — the place to attend extravagant parties and eat Sunday curry tiffin lunches.

The Japanese High Command used the hotel as its headquarters during World War II and one officer committed suicide there with a samurai sword as the war came to an end. It is said his ghost lived in Room 48.

Before independence, it was a favourite meeting place for Malaya's blossoming political parties. The founders of the Malaysian Chinese Association, the United Malays National Organization and the Malaysian Indian Congress — today's ruling government coalition — met there to plan strategy.

Today the hotel houses 1,700 works of art, displayed in a rabbit warren of 38 small, oddly shaped former bedrooms and bathrooms. The lack of air-conditioning and humidity control concerns some artists who worry about fungus damaging their works. The gallery also has two central airwells that let in sunlight and rain, adding to the technical problems.

Despite its drawbacks, artists say the Majestic is a great improvement over the Tunku Abdul Rahman mansion, which housed the gallery for 25 years. Today the gallery attracts international exhibits and the number of visitors keeps increasing.

Inside the new gallery, there is no reference to the Majestic Hotel or its past. There's no room for such memorabilia, the gallery director says, adding "Sometimes the history can better be remembered by the memory than the actual thing."

Lat's Lot

Mohammad Nor Khalid's business card is a self-portrait — a naked child dancing in front of a wooden house. In Malaysia, Mohammad Nor is better known as Lat, probably Southeast Asia's best loved and most widely read cartoonist.

Since 1974, when he joined the New Straits Times, he has, in fact, caused a revolution in Malaysian cartooning, going "from a time when you are scared to draw the prime minister to a time you can draw the prime minister looking like a fool," says Lat.

But it is by drawing the poignant, gleeful and tender moments of life in the kampung that Lat has endeared himself to Malaysia and to the world. His simple drawings are a mirror for his people. They show the the disappearance of village life.

The young boys in Lat's books get government jobs in Kuala Lumpur, adopt long haircuts and designer clothes and spend weekends in Penang — not at the kampung.

"You can't go back to it anymore. It's gone forever. You can't drink the water in the stream anymore — it's dirty ... I got several letters from people who say they cried, which I don't like. You shouldn't cry. You are supposed to laugh," he says.

"Tourists always come here and they look at the houses on stilts, but they don't know who lives in there," he says. "What kind of people? What kind of religion do they have? Have they got traditions? They see naked children running around ... I was one of those children"

His nickname comes from "bulat," the Malay word for round. He is. He is also disarmingly frank. He began drawing at seven and by 13 — after many rejections — he sold a 24-page comic book. His early characters were from movies — John Wayne and kris-brandishing warriors from the old Malay sultanate of Malacca. Influenced by English comics Beano and Dandy, he drew Western-looking people with Malay names.

By 17 he was producing a weekly comic for a local newspaper and after a disastrous high school career he headed straight for the newspaper in Kuala Lumpur. But cartoonists were not in demand, and instead he was made a reporter. One night he took newspapers to the morgue at 3 a.m. "There was nobody there. I said, 'Hello, hello.' ... It was very frightening. I threw away the papers and ran." He was a reporter for four years but he felt he never got any better.

His big break came when Asia Magazine published a cartoon on Lat's own circumcision. Before it was printed his father — dubious of his son's career — had died. Soon he was hired as a cartoonist for the New Straits Times.

Many of his characters are real — his heavy-set father and his fierce schoolteacher with butterfly glasses — and young cartoonists have begun to imitate him. "I have to tell these fellows, this is my father, don't draw." His women are fat and their husbands skinny because Lat always wants the woman to win. "If there's any problem, she can always hit him on the head."

On Becoming Malaysian

As the British retreated from the Japanese in 1941, Malayan civil servant Mervyn Sheppard organized a guerrilla group to fight behind enemy lines. But after a bout with typhus, he ended up in Singapore's Changi Prison instead. There he was caught passing a military message and was tortured.

"I was slightly mad. I think later on I would have been killed, but I was lucky. You see, this was quite early on and so the Japanese thought they were winning," he said. After the war, he evened the score. He collected a few Indian troops and a boat from a collaborator who was hoping for leniency and began chasing down fleeing Japanese in nearby islands. Eventually he captured about 700 with more military help.

"I suddenly realized that the thing I had to do was to go and chase the Japanese. So I did ... I was always known as a bloody nuisance," he recalled.

Sheppard, now in his eighties, came to Malaya in 1928 as a civil service cadet after graduating with honours from Cambridge. When Malaya received its indepedence in 1957, he was one of a handful of British men who stayed behind to become Malaysians.

Today he is considered the country's authority on traditional Malay crafts, drama and dance and he has written 17 books. He founded the Information Department, the National Archives, the National Museum, and the National Art Gallery. He insisted the museum be designed in traditional Malay architecture — a unique idea that has since become popular.

During the Emergency of the 1950s, he organized central rice kitchens in resettled areas and rubber estates to serve cooked rice, thereby preventing the large scale smuggling of uncooked rice to communists. By 1957, 53,000 people were fed this way and the rate of communists surrendering had tripled. He also used a Malay magician to charm a notorious communist into surrendering — without official approval.

When Independence came, Sheppard had to decide whether to stay in Malaysia or to move back to a 40-room Irish castle and 400 hectares of farm land. His Irish family tree includes a speaker of the Irish House of Commons, a Lord of the Treasury and a Provost of Trinity College, Dublin. In 1957 he gave up the name Mervyn, which had been passed down in the Sheppard family in alternative generations since 1700. Mervyn Sheppard became a Malaysian and a Muslim and changed his name to Mubin, an Arabic name.

"Eventually I decided converting was the logical thing to do if I was going to stay here," Sheppard said. "My father and all my ancestors are very Protestant, Low Church — minimum of ceremony, absolutely no incense, no vestments, very plain. It is the easiest thing to switch from Low Church, Church of Ireland to Islam. Both believe in one God, that's basic."

During a pilgrimage to Mecca, he was inspired to start an organization to spread Islam, especially to Chinese. In 15 years, 20,000 Malaysian Chinese were converted.

He was given the title of Tan Sri by the king after organising a Southeast Asian cultural festival soon after the May 13, 1969 riots. He wanted to show that "the capital of Malaysia is not such a desperate place as people think it is."

In his memoirs, he dubbed himself an "unorthodox civil servant".

sinated in Perak in 1875, has been renamed to honour the man who ordered Birch's killing, Maharaja Lela. Many of the colonial mansions built by Chinese *towkays* with circular verandahs and heavy Roman columns have been converted to schools or storage bins for the rusty reinforcing steel needed for adjacent high-rises under construction.

It has been said that "The two most important things in Malaysia are religion and

tubs and sugar cane is pulled through a washing machine-style wringer for its green juice. The feet of butchered pigs stick out into the aisles. Malay Muslims, forbidden by the Koran to eat pork, scurry around the pig section.

In Chow Kit Market, Malays deep-fry *chempedak* fruit and doughy bananas in bright orange batter and grind blocks of ice for *ice kacang*, a snow-cone sitting on beans and black jelly cubes and topped with red syrup and

food." The *kedai kopi*, coffee shop, is the heart of every neighbourhood. Politics, love, revenge, and money are all discussed over formica tables as the drink concessionaire brings large frosty bottles of Anchor beer and the noodle man carries in bowls of steaming *mee hoon*. The *satay* vendor brings barbequed meat on bamboo skewers with spicy peanut sauce and cubes of cold compressed rice, *ketupat*, wrapped in braided coconut leaves. Stingray flesh, rubbed with bright yellow tumeric powder and grilled on a banana leaf, is sold by another mini-vendor.

The markets are alive with Malay, Chinese and Indian hawkers. Here frogs are skinned alive, two-foot monitor lizards lie on the butcher block, live crickets are sold for feeding singing birds, and US$1,000 Golden Dragon fish, which bring good luck, are for sale. Snowy-white soybean curd is scooped out of wooden

thick condensed milk. During the day the street is packed with bicycle grocery carts under umbrellas. The garbage truck comes by, the carts roll back; the truck leaves, the carts fill in like a South China Sea wave wiping out the pattern of sand crabs.

"Chicken, chicken, very cheap. Hurry, hurry. If you're late, you'll miss out," hawkers shout rapid-fire like auctioneers to indifferent customers. Chartreuse ladies' fingers and red chillies are precisely laid out in blue and red plastic bowls. A photograph is taken. But then the hawker notices one ladies' finger out of place and reaches down to line it up with the others in a neat arrangement.

Colourful awnings (left) shade the market at Crab Island in a town built on stilts over the water. At Chinatown's long established Hai Soon Leong wholesalers (above), workers sift small dried fish, or ikan bilis, on the sidewalk.

At night these carts disappear and others take their place. The crackle and smoke of *satay* fires fill the air, coconut sweets are steamed in bamboo tubes, and chestnuts are roasted with black rocks in large *woks* or frying pans. The city throbs at night. Kerosene lanterns and neon signs burn brightly, rows of blue jeans and imitation designer shirts hang from makeshift stalls, and medicine men with fat, docile snakes sit on the ground promising miracle cures into microphones.

Stalls serve thick, dark local coffee. Before grinding, the coffee beans are fried with margarine and sugar in large *woks*. The ground coffee is then steeped in boiling water and strained through conical cloth bags. In Indian stalls, pulled tea, *teh tarik*, is mixed with sweetened condensed milk. The tea is poured from a great height between fat enamel cups until it foams like a milkshake.

Roti canai, the closest thing to a national bread, is thrown like a pizza in the air, then expertly folded together and fried on a large black griddle. When toasted, the *rotis* are stacked and slapped together, producing vigorous explosions of steam in the Indian cook's face. To go with it, dhal or spicy curry sauce, is poured into a small plastic bag, a rubber band is adeptly snapped in place and the whole meal is wrapped in a newspaper. Breakfast is ready. It is impossible to stop at one.

Fresh coconut water, soybean milk or red rose syrup are dumped into small plastic bags with ice. Full bags — hung up by workers until break time — decorate fences and plants like exotic fruit. In herbal stores, shark's fins and deer antlers are gift wrapped in plastic boxes tied with red ribbons. Tiger, deer, and seal genitals are also available to increase virility.

Durians, a fat, spiky green fruit, are sold everywhere. They are smelled, felt and consumed with ardour by men and women who crouch on street curbs sucking the white creamy fruit. Described as caramel custard with a garbage pit smell, durians are forbidden in some hotels because what is the smell of ambrosia to some is stench to others. Highly prized, they have been traded for drugs, *dadah*, in some quarters and are reputed to be the only fruit a tiger desires. The fruit's aphrodisiac properties inspired the saying, "When the durians come down, the *sarongs* go up."

***Night shoppers** throng the street where Chow Kit Market spills onto Jalan Tuanku Abdul Rahman. Street vendors sell towels, steamed coconut sweets, and fast food dinners to the late night crowd.*

Popular singer Sudirman, centre, entertains a packed audience at K.L.'s Stadium Merdeka. Some conservative youths had protested earlier pop music perform-ances, saying Sudirman represented corrupting western influences. But this crowd loves his antics. An international marathon preceded the performance.

The city's people barely pause in their eating and buying to acknowledge the almost-daily rains. There is a brisk wind, the sky blackens, the rain pours down in torrents and lightning strikes, all in a few minutes. China-town shoppers continue doing business under the painted bamboo shades that permanently cover sidewalks. Street vendors hoist up large yellow, blue and red umbrellas over their wheeled fruit carts. The alleyway stall owners put out buckets to catch the water to wash their fish and vegetables.

The motorcyclists pause on the highways to don plastic mackintoshes or leather jackets — reversed, the collars up over their mouths. If the rain is heavy, they stop under flyovers to wait it out. *Amahs* rush to pull in the laundry, which must be on the line early in the morning to dry before the afternoon rains. Often within 20 minutes, the heavy rain is over and business

continues. The air smells fresher, the streets washed clean, the open gutters less malignant. Mist rises from the pavement.

The signs and symbols of religion abound. With large communities of devout Hindus, Buddhists, Christians and Muslims, religious festivals seem non-ending. The New Year alone is honoured four times a year. Faith is part of daily life. From minarets all over the city, the *bilal* calls Muslims to prayer five times a day. The government-run television chan-nels also broadcast the call and the exact times are printed in the radio and television guide.

Malaysia, caught between a resurgence of Islamic fundamentalism and more liberal

Honouring a Hindu goddess. A Malaysian Bengali Association dancer (above) performs a traditional dance. While the Batu Caves Art Gallery (right) illustrates the story of Lord Subramaniam killing the demon Suran with a spear.

views, faces a dilemma. Indians and Chinese, with their own religious and political views, make up almost half the population, creating a country that must maintain a careful balancing act. Religious freedom is the mainstay of the Malaysian government.

To demonstrate their faith, young Muslim women have currently taken to wearing mini-*telekungs*, veils that cover the hair and neck and drop down to the waist. The veils have become almost a national dress among Malay school children. The most conservative Muslim women, commonly called *dakwahs*, wear gloves and cover themselves completely in dark cloth, leaving only their eyes visible. The government is curtailing the dress in the universities and civil service.

Muslim women often shun nail polish and hair dye because they prevent water from touching the skin during cleansing for daily

prayers. Instead *inai*, or henna, a natural red dye, is used to cover greying hair and to decorate nails and feet for weddings. Friday mornings, the modern National Mosque filled with men wearing black *songkok* caps and plaid *sarongs*. Women pray at home.

The men check their shoes at the door for 20 *sen* — a new service for the safety conscious — and then perform the ritual washing of five parts of the body. Inside the men stand in rows, then touch their foreheads four times to long strips of cloth laid across the carpeted floor.

The few women who attend on other days slip into white prayer dresses that cover from head to foot and sit a distance behind the men.

Bride Normala (left) models one of nine dresses rented for her wedding day. Her marriage was arranged so she only met her husband a month after the engagement. Going to the National Mosque (above) on special days is a family excursion.

A *bomoh* (below) uses the Koran to bring back a missing husband. Young Chinese men (left) adopt the latest fashion in hairstyles and clothes.

Malaysia's Ghostbusters

The Malaysian Golf Association has used a bomoh, a Malay medicine man, to ward off rain during major tournaments for nearly 15 years. On more than one occasion, the rain poured — just after the last ball was sunk to the awe of Western golfers.

"If I stick my neck out and say, 'Let's forget about the bomoh, and it pours cats and dogs, they will say, 'Why didn't you get him?'' says an Association spokesman who does not believe it works.

For a country steeped in Islamic beliefs, the widespread acceptance of ancient magic illustrates an interesting paradox. For while Kuala Lumpur is a modern metropolis, a tenacious belief in vampires, devils and other assorted ghosts thrives.

According to one retired government worker, "The bomoh can cure all disease except death." Bomohs claim they are regularly sought out by Malays, Chinese and Indians alike for such tasks as curing high blood pressure and diabetes, terminating pregnancies, driving off cobras, preventing robberies, and returning errant husbands and making them faithful.

The bomoh is Malaysia's real-life ghostbuster. Since prehistoric times, bomohs and animistic beliefs have held sway in Malay life. Despite the spread of Buddhism, Hinduism and finally Islam during the past 1,700 years, bomohs have continued to survive by skillfully adapting to each religion. Both bomohs who perform harmless tasks and those who practice black magic — unacceptable to most Malays — rely on verses from the Koran and claim to be good Muslims. They say verses of the Koran have an additional meaning which is very powerful and known only to bomohs who generally inherit their skills from ancestors.

There are an estimated 4,000 male and female bomohs in Malaysia today. Some have received bad press in the past few years for allegedly swindling customers, raping patients and even causing death.

But many bomohs today act much like conventional doctors. They attend conferences at universities to discuss the latest cures; they form organisations to discipline unethical practitioners; they specialise.

Bomohs have also tackled high tech. A number of international electronics companies in Malaysia were plagued by problems with hysteria in the 1970s when 50 incidents were reported. A young female worker would see a ghost through a microscope and fall down screaming. Other workers would follow suit. Several companies brought in bomohs to sacrifice goats and say verses from the Koran. The incidents then ceased. One executive said he had difficulty explaining to his American head office why he needed several hundred ringgits for bomohs and goats.

One Kuala Lumpur bomoh claims to have cured 4,000 morphine and heroin addicts in the past nine years with only a one per cent recidivisim rate. He writes Koran verses on the addict's back and chest and gives him spiritual baths to chase out the evil spirit that possesses him.

The country's revered first prime minister, Tunku Abdul Rahman, wrote in his weekly newspaper column that a bomoh once cured his tennis shoulder by rubbing a cane in the correct place. The Tunku also complained about a slipped disc that Western medicine had failed to cure, and asked his readers for a referral, as if to say that visiting a good bomoh can't hurt.

When the mosque is crowded on the birthday of the Prophet Mohammad, women and children sit on the upper floor and watch the men through decorative grilles. Children play patty-cake to pass the time but during prayer, they cup their hands in reverence. The song-like prayer of the *imams* fill the grounds from a loudspeaker.

Muslims fast once a year during the month of Ramadan, the ninth month in the Muslim

calendar. An unusual quiet settles over Kuala Lumpur. Muslims awaken before 5 a.m. to eat before the sun rises and do not take food or drink until the sun sets. The night before the new moon is expected again, women cook dry curry beef, *beef rendang*, glutinous rice cooked with coconut milk in bamboo, *lemang*, and red seaweed jelly, *agar agar*, until the wee hours.

Hari Raya Puasa, the day after fasting ends, is similar in form to the Christian Christmas. Hari Raya means Happy Day and cards are sent to friends, open houses are held throughout the city for people of all faiths, and the king, prime minister and top leaders shake hands and feed anyone who comes calling.

A Hindu devotee (above) spears his cheeks at Thaipusam but pulls the spear out shortly after in apparent pain. Some believers with long hair walk on swords and smoke cigars. This ceremony begins at the Sri Maha Mariamman Temple (right).

On any day one can see Indian women, elegantly dressed in *saris* with yards of flowing material, buying coral flowers for their hair from the broad-bottomed street vendor who sits for hours, stringing together cassandra and jasmine. They perspire through tight, short-sleeved blouses that stop two fleshy rolls short of their waistlines. Brightly coloured Hindu temples are decorated with delicately intertwined coconut leaves and hanging banana flowers for a wedding. The groom wears a thick garland of heady flowers that often takes up to four hours to weave and the bride hesitates before moving — her forehead, ears, nose, feet, arms, fingers studded with gold rings, diamonds and glitter.

Hindus enter the temple barefoot and dip a finger into a powder made from scarlet vermilion, sandalwood paste and grey ash from cow dung that reportedly has never touched the ground. The powder is put on the forehead to represent the third eye of Shiva.

Once a year at Thaipusam half a million pilgrims throng Batu Caves outside the city to carry *kavadis* — large metal frames decorated with peacock feathers, pictures of deities and symbolic dolls — up the 272 steps of the cave to show devotion to Lord Subramaniam. Devotees fall into deep trances, their cheeks are pierced with five-foot spears, and fruit or pots

The Chong Yun Long opera performs for an audience at Sun Hoon Keong, an unpretentious temple in a small home. The Malaysian opera company, with Hong Kong trained performers, costs about US$5,000 for seven evenings of entertainment. The temple is known for its miraculous healings and fire walking, sword climbing and hot oil ceremonies.

of milk are hung from hooks dug into their chests and backs. Some brandish swords threateningly. Usually there is no pain or scars and little blood is shed.

In the heart of Kuala Lumpur, a Chinese funeral is announced by the loud thump of drums as sackcloth-dressed mourners — both paid wailers and family members — parade in the street after a boat shaped coffin, hewn from mammoth *yinchemui* logs. A photograph of

Later in the year, a less peaceful ceremony occurs at the Kau Ong Yah Temple in Kampung Ampang when the Nine Emperor Gods are honoured. The nine days of celebrating begin with believers piercing their cheeks with metal rods and cutting their backs with butcher knives while in a trance. The celebration ends with a crowded firewalking ceremony. Some walkers carry tea on their backs and sell it later for a high price.

the deceased leans against the coffin and whole glazed pigs are set out in full view as an offering to the gods.

Large drooping incense coils fill the entrance of the Chinese temples with smoke. Inside worshippers shake sticks out of cylinders to learn the answers to practical questions and give offerings of joss sticks and lamp oil to improve prospects for passing examinations, being promoted, or winning the lottery.

To celebrate Lord Buddha's birthday on Vesak Day, Buddhist monks in saffron robes sprinkle holy water on believers, who kneel in prayer before a flower strewn, red-lipped Buddha. At the International Buddhist Pagoda centre in Brickfields, visitors wait in line to kiss the face of the giant reclining Buddha. Nuns, with shaven heads and wearing long black robes, lead a procession of children in the massive candle-light parade.

Centuries-old sports and hobbies still abide in Kuala Lumpur today. On some days, men "walk" their birds in elaborately carved cages from China. The *merbuk* and other prized singing birds, costing up to US$12,000, are pampered for their voices and ability to bring businessmen luck. Originally an Indonesian pastime, bird singing competitions are held regularly. The birds are hoisted up seven-metre poles and meticulously judged. The tall poles eliminate distracting sounds and birds just sing better higher up, say organizers. In one incident, a US$5,000 *merbuk* was injured, its singing voice possibly destroyed, when wind toppled its five and a half metre pole.

At a Chinese crematorium, paper luxuries are burned for the dead to use in the spirit world (left and above). A Kelantan bird kite, or wau burung, is on display at the National Museum and a batik print is painted at Kutang Kraft (following pages).

In preparation for competitions, the birds are sunned daily, bathed once a week, and given small hot chillies to clear the throat. By counting the leg scales, the owner can determine whether the bird is lucky and which part of the house to keep it in. Bad luck birds can destroy a marriage or a business.

Another sport played in school yards and back lots is *sepak takraw*, a type of volley ball game with a rattan ball. But the rule is "no hands." The players, looking like ballet dancers, are frozen by the camera in mid-air as their legs slice over the net with amazing agility. The 15th century royal sport is played at Southeast Asian sports competitions where Malaysia is often the winner.

A major street, Jalan Gasing, is named after a predominantly east coast sport, top spinning. Originally played in *padi*, or rice, growing regions, top spinning at cultural shows also

draws crowds in Kuala Lumpur who eagerly watch muscled men throwing hardwood discs weighing up to six kilograms. The best players keep a top spinning for more than an hour.

Kite flying, also a favourite in the eastern states of Kelantan and Trengganu, is such a part of Malaysian culture that bird-shaped kites decorate residential walls and stores throughout the city and form the symbol for Malaysia's national airline. Another ancient artifact, the small wavy dagger called the *kris*, has also become part of the city's decor. Artisans can still be found who hammer a *kris* from many metals — even a bicycle chain — and carve fine ivory and silver handles. The

Indonesian puppets (left) are carved by Javanese rubber estate workers in Malaysia. The shadow play, or wayang kulit *(above), is the oldest theatre form in much of Southeast Asia. The plays are based on a 2,000-year-old Hindu epic.*

razor-sharp *kris*, was a common weapon in the 15th century when it was believed to harbour a magical spirit. Some scholars say it is the only major weapon indigenous to Southeast Asia.

There are numerous *kampungs* or villages within the city today that give one a glimpse into rural life. Many are called squatter villages because the residents have built their shelters illegally while waiting for government housing. Nearly one-fourth of the city lives in such areas. Inside the Muslim homes, floors are covered with patterned linoleum and walls are decorated with framed Koran verses and velvet paintings of mosques. Many houses have full glass cupboards displaying the plentiful dishware used for important occasions — births, circumcisions, weddings, Hari Raya, and deaths. Televisions, sometimes run by car batteries, are considered a necessity. Many such settlements are now being replaced by

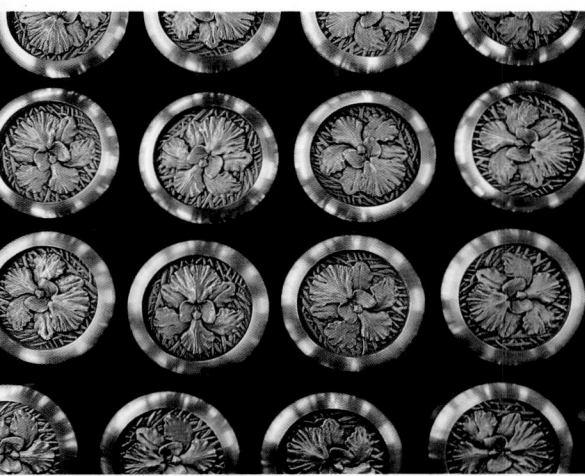

high-rise concrete blocks of flats.

Outdoor hawker stalls are also being moved inside high-rises. However, some will remain, such as the Hilton Drive-in, which isn't a drive-in and isn't in the Hilton, although its employees are reputed to eat there. The Drive-in has been promised piped water and electricity. Workers will be required to wear matching uniforms, caps and name tags. Their lifestyle is vanishing like the wealth of tin under Kuala Lumpur's feet. In its place is a city reaching into the future yet conscious of its heritage. Its diverse and fascinating people, representing a rare amalgam of cultures, will keep it colourful.

*Orchid-designed **pewter pill boxes (above)** and copper Trengganu batik blocks **(right)** form colourful patterns. The blocks are dipped in wax, then carefully laid on fabric to form a pattern.*

Magic Daggers

The kris, *a double-edged dagger with a reputation for magical properties, is the most significant historical weapon in Malaysia and Indonesia.*

It is an essential part of royal attire for ceremonial occasions, but even the poorest Malay groom will wear one to his wedding when he is "raja for a day". A miniature kris *is put in a bowl of water and used to conjure lucky lottery numbers at the Petaling Street night market.* Kris *letter openers are in vogue.*

Believed to have originated in Java, the kris *was an essential 15th century weapon and even as late as the 19th century, no adult Malay male would leave his house without one. Nor is it without its 20th-century uses. In a 1985 election squabble in Sabah, a top official grabbed for his* kris, *he said, when he felt his life threatened.*

The short dagger was designed for a horizontal thrust and for fighting in narrow streets. A longer narrow straight kris *was used in executions — thrust in front of the left collarbone down to the heart. Some warriors carried both a long and short* kris.

The most common Malay kris *has a 28 cm. blade with seven sinuous, lethal curves. The hilt is usually in the shape of a bird's head, unlike Indonesian* kris *that have Hindu figures on the hilt.*

The hilt is grasped in the same way as the butt of a pistol. One theory is that the weapon may have been inspired by the double-barbed sting of a stingray fish. An actual sting, shaved down as if it had been fitted to a handle, has been found at one ancient site.

It was believed that some kris *had supernatural powers. When cleaning the blade, owners had to pass it through benzoin smoke or it would rattle in the sheath at night. A* kris *that had drawn a lot of blood was believed to make its owner invulnerable. Bomohs, or medicine men, have been known to "draw water" from a* kris *blade, a sleight-of-hand trick that is said to ruin the blade.*

Early Malaysian hilts were often carved with the figure of a Hindu deity or a Garuda, an animal with the head of a bird and body of a man. With the introduction of Islam, these Hindu figures were considered sacrilegious. However, kris-makers *retained some of their original images with the hope that Hindu deities would still abide in them — thus giving their owners assurance in both religions.*

The most decorative hilt had the shape of a mystical bird's head and was called the Kingfisher Head Kris. Most kris *are tucked into a front waistband, but this* kris *was so long it had to be worn at the back. If attacked, the owner would kick the shaft with his heel and grab the hilt when it reached shoulder level. If the attacker was too close to stab, the bird's beak could be pushed into his eye, effectively blinding him.*

Back of the Book

This back of the book section was designed to help you push your travel experience further by informing, enlightening and entertaining you as you continue your exploration of Kuala Lumpur. There are maps of central K.L. and environs. Little known facts about K.L. — like why Pudu Prison made it into the 1986 Guiness Book of Records — are revealed in *K.L. Trivia.* Suggested tours, with helpful maps, take you around the Padang, through Chinatown, to a market, around the shops and on a tour of the city's early architecture. *Off the Beaten Track* tells you where to go to see Malaysia's largest and most elaborate Chinese temple and how to take a day trip to a peaceful nearby island, amongst other interesting and unusual places to visit and things to try. *Best Bets* has a listing of the best K.L. has to offer — from batik, dim sum and children's entertainment to cane furniture, conversation pieces, views and food stalls. *Travel Notes* gives you the travel "basics".

The city softened by the soft early evening light (left). The Sime Darby corporate headquarters glow in the setting sun on Jalan Raja Laut.

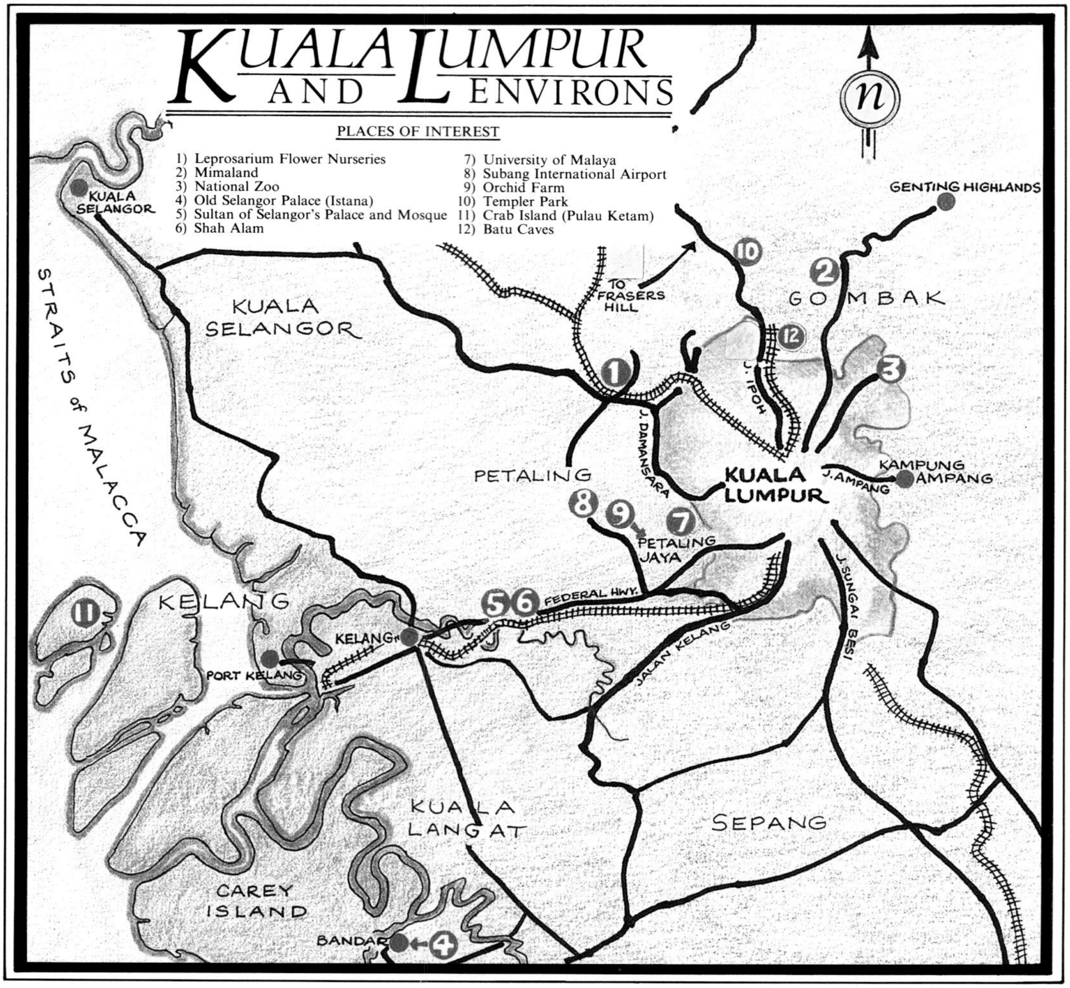
KUALA LUMPUR AND ENVIRONS
PLACES OF INTEREST
1) Leprosarium Flower Nurseries
2) Mimaland
3) National Zoo
4) Old Selangor Palace (Istana)
5) Sultan of Selangor's Palace and Mosque
6) Shah Alam
7) University of Malaya
8) Subang International Airport
9) Orchid Farm
10) Templer Park
11) Crab Island (Pulau Ketam)
12) Batu Caves
n
GENTING HIGHLANDS
KUALA SELANGOR
STRAITS of MALACCA
KUALA SELANGOR
TO FRASERS HILL
GOMBAK
J. IPOH
J. DAMANSARA
PETALING
KUALA LUMPUR
KAMPUNG AMPANG
J. AMPANG
PETALING JAYA
FEDERAL HWY.
J. SUNGAI BESI
KELANG
KELANG
PORT KELANG
JALAN KELANG
KUALA LANGAT
SEPANG
CAREY ISLAND
BANDAR

MALAYSIA IN THE REGION
PHILLIPINES
PENANG
MALAYSIA
STRAITS OF MALACCA
KUALA LUMPUR
MALACCA
SINGAPORE
SUMATRA
KOTA KINABALU
SABAH
BRUNEI
SARAWAK
MALAYSIA
KUCHING
CELEBES SEA
KALIMANTAN (BORNEO)
SULAWESI
PALEMBANG
INDONESIA
JAVA SEA
JAKARTA
INDIAN OCEAN

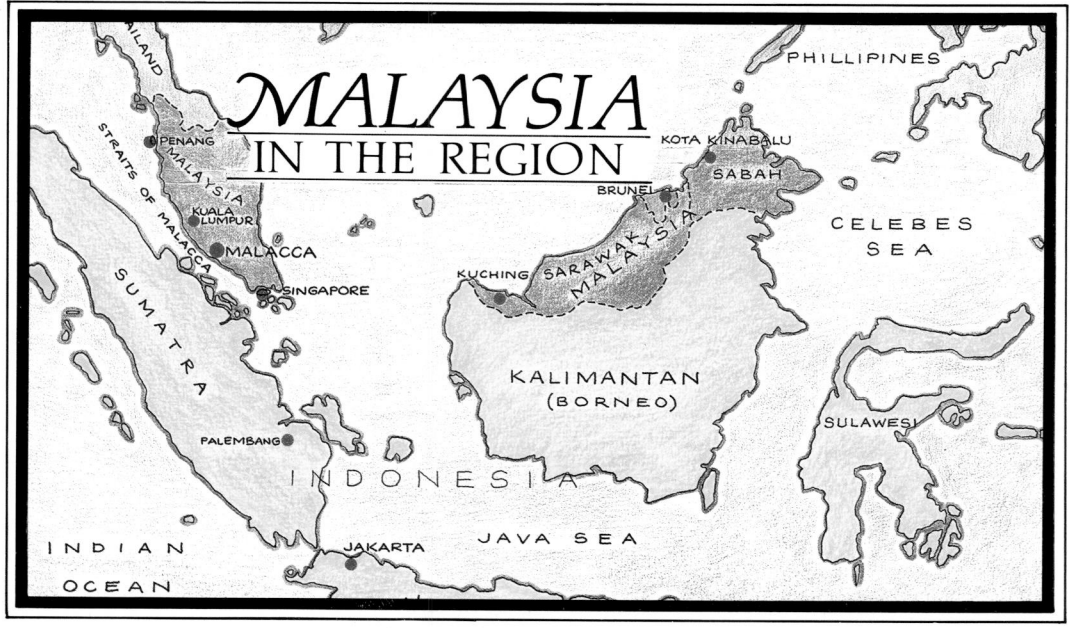

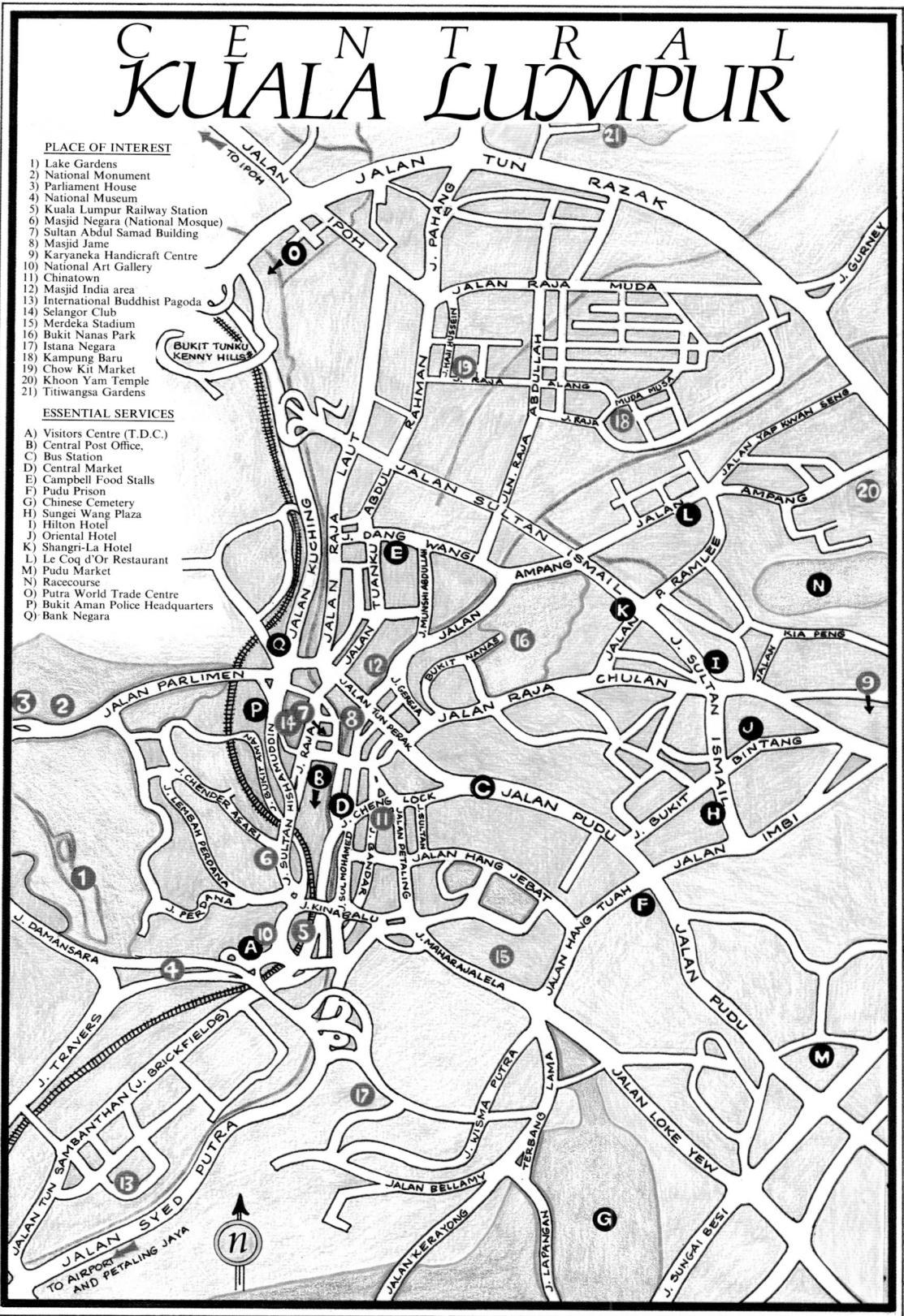

CENTRAL
KUALA LUMPUR

PLACE OF INTEREST
1) Lake Gardens
2) National Monument
3) Parliament House
4) National Museum
5) Kuala Lumpur Railway Station
6) Masjid Negara (National Mosque)
7) Sultan Abdul Samad Building
8) Masjid Jame
9) Karyaneka Handicraft Centre
10) National Art Gallery
11) Chinatown
12) Masjid India area
13) International Buddhist Pagoda
14) Selangor Club
15) Merdeka Stadium
16) Bukit Nanas Park
17) Istana Negara
18) Kampung Baru
19) Chow Kit Market
20) Khoon Yam Temple
21) Titiwangsa Gardens

ESSENTIAL SERVICES
A) Visitors Centre (T.D.C.)
B) Central Post Office,
C) Bus Station
D) Central Market
E) Campbell Food Stalls
F) Pudu Prison
G) Chinese Cemetery
H) Sungei Wang Plaza
I) Hilton Hotel
J) Oriental Hotel
K) Shangri-La Hotel
L) Le Coq d'Or Restaurant
M) Pudu Market
N) Racecourse
O) Putra World Trade Centre
P) Bukit Aman Police Headquarters
Q) Bank Negara

K.L. Trivia

UNREQUITED LOVE. Every visitor to Kuala Lumpur hears the story of unrequited love associated with Le Coq d'Or, a run-down colonial mansion turned restaurant. It is one of the last Chinese mansions still standing on Jalan Ampang because owner-builder Chua Cheng Bok decreed in his will the mansion not be sold nor could the interior be changed. As a young man, the story goes, Chua fell in love. But because he was poor, his true love's father refused to let the couple marry. In retribution, he worked hard, became wealthy and built a mansion across from the unrelenting father. The house overshadowed that of the father and cut him off from the forces of good fortune. Unfortunately, an estate spokesman says there is not a word of truth in it.

PRISON WALLS. Kuala Lumpur's Pudu Prison made the Guinness Book of Records in 1986 for having the most decorative prison walls, measuring 262 metres long. The year before, the prison was cited for having the longest mural. Four prisoners painted the tropical scene. During the painting, prisoners escaped over the palm-decorated wall and through the new rock gardens. Later four more prisoners escaped through a guard house being redesigned in elaborate Malay style.

MERDEKA RECORD. The Merdeka Day celebration in Kuala Lumpur in 1982 holds the Guinness record for having the largest marching band with 2,560 musicians.

EMPTY TANKARD. Selangor Pewter created the world's largest pewter beer tankard, with a capacity of 2,660 litres, for their centennial in 1985. It took six workers 2,000 hours to make it. The beer mug has not been filled because the beer would go stale.

LARGEST DOME. Southeast Asia's largest domed mosque, Masjid Sultan Salahuddin, was completed in 1986 in the Kuala Lumpur suburb of Shah Alam. The mosque's dome is 51 metres in diameter and 92 metres in height, making it larger than St. Paul's Cathedral in London, and possibly the largest religious dome in the world. It may also be the most expensive.

NOTORIOUS RAILWAY. During the Japanese occupation several Malaysian railway lines were transported to Burma for the notorious Siam-Burma railway, the site of the book, *The Bridge on the River Kwai*, which was made into one of the moviedom's best-loved films with Alec Guinness.

THE CHETTIES. A south Indian caste of money-lenders, the Chetties, followed the British expansion into Malaya and held the monopoly on cash credit — charging 36 per cent interest — for many years. The Chetties reported they had loaned a total of $100 million to peasants in the Federated Malay States by 1930. When the government saw Malays and other peasants losing their land, it rushed through laws limiting foreclosure. But Chetties can still be seen today working as money lenders in Kuala Lumpur.

LOVE LETTER. Somerset Maugham's short story, "The Letter" stems from one of Malaysia's most celebrated scandals. In 1911 Mrs. Ethel Proudlock, wife of the acting headmaster of Kuala Lumpur's top secondary school the Victoria Institution, shot and killed a European she said was attempting to rape her. The man was a consulting engineer, who the prosecution implied was Mrs. Proudlock's lover. The truth was never discovered but Mrs. Proudlock was convicted and sentenced to be hanged — causing a great uproar in the European community, which believed her innocent. The sultan granted a pardon and Mrs. Proudlock left for England. In the Maugham version the wife is acquitted and the letter, which would have convicted her, is destroyed. Hollywood turned it into a movie starring Bette Davis.

HASH HOUSE HARRIERS. In 1938, four British men living in a Selangor Club annex called the Hash House because of its institutional food, organized a run through the jungle. They called themselves the Hash House Harriers. Today the Hash, as it is called, is one of Kuala Lumpur's most enduring social events and has become an international phenomenon as well. There are six clubs in the Kuala Lumpur area — with about 500 members, 65 clubs in Malaysia, and possibly 400 worldwide. A person called a hare lays a paper trail for his mates to follow through the jungle, then provides a large supply of post-run beer.

DURIAN LORE. Alcohol and durian should not be consumed together, according to Chinese belief, because they are both "heaty" foods and would unbalance the *yin-yang* and cause illness. Durian milkshakes were all the rage at McDonald's for a while. .Afficionados say the best way to eat durian is all-out — eating four fruits a person — and then not eat it again for a year. To eliminate the smell, run water over the shell then over your hands and use it for a mouth wash.

CLOSE PROXIMITY. Unmarried couples who kiss or are found in secluded places in Malaysia can be charged by the religious department with *khalwat* or "close proximity." Former Prime Minister Tunku Abdul Rahman wrote in his newspaper column of one famed case in which a 104-year-old man plead guilty to a charge of *khalwat*, possibly to boast of his prowess. "Why not leave him alone, for he has little to live for and there is not much left of life for him," the father of the country wrote. He noted, "Thousands commit *khalwat*, some do so intentionally and some unintentionally, but they all enjoy doing it."

PAPERLESS TOILET. The Malaysian government in 1984 invented the paperless Islamic toilet to market to one billion Muslims around the world. The toilet has a spout that produces a high-pressure stream of warm water, eliminating the need for paper. The new Pan Pacific Hotel and Putra World Trade Centre were the first public buildings to install the toilets.

OILY MAN. For more than half a century the *orang minyak*, or oily man, has haunted women's bedrooms in Malaysia and Singapore. The man wears only a pair of shorts and is covered with oil. He can squeeze through a crack, suck women's blood, and change into a frog or insect, observers say. Some believe he has a Thai magical charm that makes him invisible to men. He also does evil things to girls, not specified in the newspapers, has committed robberies and terrorized whole communities. In Kuala Lumpur he hangs around Jalan Imbi, but is too slippery to catch.

CRADLE ROCK. The traditional Malay baby cradle, a *sarong* suspended so it can be rocked, has been mechanized by Japan. The electronic baby cradle, which sells for around M$365, rocks the *sarong* for up to 12 hours and plays 16 tunes including Brahms' lullaby. Promoters say the cradle prevents the baby's head from being flattened, improves the "quality of married life" by giving parents more time together, and helps working mothers get a good night's rest in accordance with "the government campaign on productivity." The cradle is not catching on.

MAD SAILORS AND ENGLISHMEN. In Malaysia, a white person is likely to be called a *mat salleh*, derived from the name "mad sailor," given to English sailors who went crazy in port. Other names for Westerners include *orang putih*, or white person in *Bahasa* Malaysia. There is another name, heard wherever there are colonies of overseas Chinese. It is *Kwai lo* (pronounced gwai low) for foreign devil in Chinese — not always a pejorative term.

TODDY BARS. Peninsular Malaysia has more than 200 toddy bars that serve a coconut tree sap for 50 *sens* a mug — called the Malaysian champagne. It is considered the poor man's drink. Toddy shops were started by the British to serve the poor Tamil plantation workers, according to a government official. Today the shops are run by the government and the estates — there are eight in Kuala Lumpur — but the government is starting to close them down. Just before the coconut palm starts to flower, the fruit's stem is cut, tied and covered with a jar to collect the sap twice a day. The sap ferments quickly so it is advisable to get to the toddy shop by 10:30 a.m. for the sweeter drink before it turns sour. Often a shop will serve 70 people a day, a regular clientele of all races but with a preponderance of Indians.

BLIND FURY. The Malay *amok*, translated by the British into the term "running amuck," is a person who broods over an insult until he seeks revenge by striking anyone he meets in a blind fury. Resident Frank Swettenham described one *amok* — a quiet, elderly religious man — who suddenly killed six people and wounded four in a few days. The National Museum has an *amok* catcher on display — a long spear with two prongs for holding the *amok* down by the neck.

MISSING LANDMARKS. The government mapping department still eliminates some landmarks — reservoirs, telecommmunications, restricted buildings and military areas — from their maps of Kuala Lumpur and other areas because of fear of communist sabotage. The 12-year Communist Emergency officially ended in 1960 although about 2,000 communist guerrillas still roam the Thai border area.

CIVIL SERVANTS. Malaysia has the largest number of public servants of any government in the free world. One person in every 17 works for the government, while in Britain one person out of every 84 is a government employee.

OVERSEAS STUDENTS. Malaysia, engaged in an intensive effort to modernize its society, had more students overseas than any other nation in the world during the mid-1980s. With only 15 million residents, in 1985 the country was the leading source of foreign university students for Britain, Australia, New Zealand and the United States.

BROKEN TAILS. Many of Malaysia's cats have bent or short tails. Some people believe the tails are broken by people who want to keep cats out of heaven because they are not part of the Chinese calendar. Others believe a cat with a broken tail won't leave him. In fact the feline defects are genetic.

KLANG RIVER. Two men spotted three crocodiles and a body while boating from K.L. to Port Klang in 1985. Three more bodies were found that week.

ROTATING ROYALTY. Malaysia is the only country in the world with rotating royalty, a system begun with Independence in 1957. The hereditary rulers of the nine states, known as sultans, vote one of their members to be king, the Yang di-Pertuan Agong. The full preferred term of address for the king is Duli Yang Maha Mulia, Sri Paduka Baginda Yang di-Pertuan Agong. Literally translated, that means "We who are below the dust under the sole of the foot of the most exalted, radiant majesty, he who is made highest in the land." But only for five years.

TIN LEGENDS. Early tin miners believed that tin ore grows and moves. A mine that yielded little was considered young. And if the spirits were not appeased, the tin would go elsewhere. It was considered a great offence to the spirits for a European to go into a mine with boots on and an opened umbrella.

KINGLY GIFT. The Malaysian king gave a rare Sumatran rhinoceros to the King of Thailand in 1985 — one of only two Sumatran rhinos in captivity in the world. The other is in the Malacca zoo.

PALM OIL. Palm oil, Malaysia's "golden crop", is used in hand soap, detergent, cosmetics, feed stock, cooking oil, lubricant, medicine, sweetened condensed milk, ice cream, and chocolates. And now there are experiments to convert it to car diesel fuel. The country is the world's largest producer of palm oil.

K.L. Tours

AROUND THE PADANG: This takes you around the most well-known buildings in Kuala Lumpur. Begin the tour at the confluence of the Klang and Gombak rivers where the early tin pioneers came ashore in 1857 and found tin overland.

Masjid Jame **(1)**, 1909, is a replica of a north Indian mosque and was built on the site of the first Malay cemetery. It was designed by British architect A.B. Hubbock who also designed the city's railway station. It has a walled courtyard and three domes flanked by two minarets. Visitors can walk around the grounds but often are not admitted into the building unless they are Muslims. It was renovated in 1984.

The Information Department **(2)**, 1909, was first used as a survey office. It was designed by A.C. Norman. Today it is an information centre where tourists can buy government maps. The old City Hall **(3)**, c. 1897, was also designed by Norman. It originally housed the Sanitary Board, the original town council. You can see the new, white city hall behind you on Jalan Raya Laut. The High Court **(4)**, 1909, still occupies this building which continues the Islamic style with a plaster facade.

The Sultan Abdul Samad Building **(5)**, 1894–97, was the first of this group. The former Selangor State Secretariat, it is now occupied by the Supreme Court. The building had numerous pinnacles but these were removed during World War II and were lost. The building was gutted and restored in 1984 to make room for the courts. Most of it is open to the public including the courtrooms. The copper domes are lacquered.

The Industrial Court Building **(6)**, c. 1905, was the city's largest department store, the Chow Kit Emporium. Loke Chow Kit began his general store in 1892 with six employees and within 16 years he had 100 workers. His clothing store was known for making modified European-style clothes for upper-class Chinese. It faced the old market.

Former General Post Office **(7)**, c. 1897. This building, also designed by Norman, is so similar to the Sultan Abdul Samad Building in the use of facing bricks that they are often viewed as one. It housed the post office until a new one was built in 1984 in the Dayabumi Complex. The Public Works Department **(8)**, 1896, originally housed the Federated Malay States Railway Headquarters. The building is scheduled to be a crafts museum.

The Chartered Bank **(9)**, c. 1909, was headquartered here for many years. The Government Printing Office **(10)**, c. 1900, was built with large windows for light. It later housed the post and telegraph offices and was renovated in 1985 with adjoining buildings.

The Selangor Club **(11)**, 1890 and 1910, commonly known as the Spotted Dog, was built in 1884 of wood and *attap* on the north side of the *padang*. The cricket field was originally a swamp until it was drained for a police training ground. A larger two-storey clubhouse was built in 1890 on the current site with the aid of a government loan. The club had 140 members in 1892 and was the centre of European social life. When the building was expanded in 1910, the second storey of the structure was removed, leaving today's one-storey half-timber building to the south. After a disastrous kitchen fire in 1970, the larger structure on the north was built. Norman also designed this Tudor-style club.

The PAM Building or Loke Hall **(12)**, 1907, was constructed by Loke Chow Kit as his home and mining offices. It was one of the finest homes in the city in the early 1900s. Loke Chow Kit took a trip to Europe in 1903 and it is believed the designs for Loke Hall and the Chow Kit Emporium were influenced by popular European styles. Notice the unusual iron work and Dutch influence. PAM, the Malaysian Institute of Architects, now acts as custodian.

The Anglo-Oriental Building **(13)**, 1936. This Art Deco building, which was restored, housed the Anglo-Oriental Mining Company and later the Malaysian Mining Corp. The Church of St. Mary the Virgin **(14)**, 1894 was the first brick Anglican Church in the Malay Peninsula. See the Father Willis organ.

You can end the tour here or walk to another historic monument, the Coliseum Cafe **(15)**, for sizzling grilled steak and fresh orange juice. Out station planters gathered here after it was built in 1920 and it is reputed to have been a favorite haunt of writer Somerset Maugham.

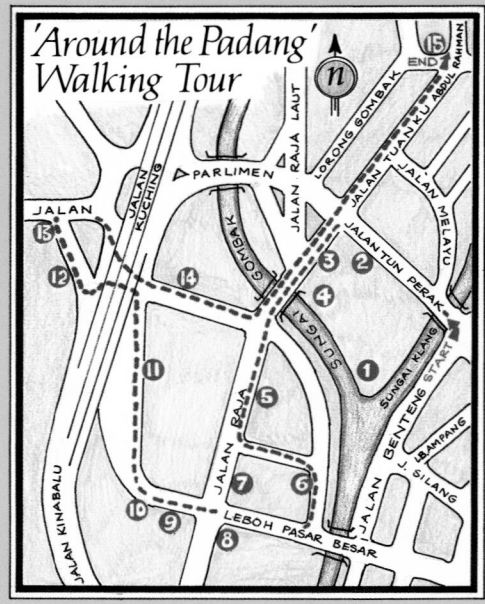

'Around the Padang' Walking Tour

AROUND CHINATOWN: This is a very alive bustling part of Kuala Lumpur where old customs and modern life blend well. Begin at the city's oldest Hindu temple, Sri Maha Mariamman Temple **(1)** on Jalan Bandar. The present structure was built in 1968 and the elaborate towers are of typical south Indian design.

On the corner is one of the narrowest coffee houses in the city, Yong Bee **(2),** which has been in the Tan family 40 years but dates back even further. As you walk farther, look up at the six 1920s shophouses **(3)** with full length wooden doors and decorative gables, and the colonial police station **(4)** next door. Behind this row of shophouses **(5)** see the U shaped airwells used for ventilation. Down the street, this rather plain wooden English cottage-style building was the Victoria Institution **(6).** Built in 1894 with leftover funds from Queen Victoria's Diamond Jubilee, it was the most successful English school in the city. The students were mostly Chinese and Indian boys who received a classical English education. The school moved to another building in 1929 and the Old Vic is now an experimental theatre needing repair.

The Tukang Jahit Soon Kee **(7)** wedding store rents Western wedding dresses. Most brides rent their gowns because to buy one costs M$600 or more. The second coffin shop down is believed to be the oldest in Kuala Lumpur. Choon Fook Coffin Shop **(8)** was opened in 1917. The original owner's grandson runs the store.

Wah Hing's funeral store **(9)** sells paper models to be burned after funerals to provide the dead with things needed in the afterlife. The roast duck shop **(10)** has been in business for about 40 years. They cook ducks for hawkers to sell on Petaling Street and will sell 40 on a good day. Ducks are blown up with a plastic pump then roasted in a smoky charcoal fire for only 20 minutes. The big drum shaped sign on the corner says Foong Wong Town Band Supplier **(11)** but the store is clearly a restaurant. In the back sits the band's saxophone player, who has been selling his band's services for 17 years especially for funerals.

Next door is Kelab Lumba Kuda Selangor **(12),** a 25-year-old gambling office. Patrons bet on the last three digits on a horse's, assigned number at the real horse races in Kuala Lumpur. A M$1 ticket can earn M$600, and on a good day 3,500 tickets are sold. Two barbers **(13)** have staked out this little piece of alley for their fold-up shop for 40 years. A haircut is M$4 and an ear cleaning is M$1. One barber handles eight customers in a day, but at night only a pile of chairs marks the barber shop on Muttiah Chetty Lane.

This hole-in-the-wall noodle factory, called Tong Tien Noodle Manufacturing **(14),** starts its work at 5 a.m. It produces excellent *wanton* skins and egg noodles. The Seng Kee Restaurant **(15)** is believed to date back to 1910 — making it one of the oldest restaurants in Kuala Lumpur. The Kaya Man **(16)** has

sold his coconut-egg custard here for 27 years. He dresses in a spotless white T-shirt and white pressed bermudas, which gives a feeling of cleanliness to his operation, and he has put six children through universities in the United States and England. This flag and banner shop **(17)** has been a family business for 30 years. For M$3 you can buy a small Malaysian flag. Restaurant Yoke Woo Hin **(18)** is known for its *dim sum* breakfast served from 6–10 a.m.

If you don't want to leave Kuala Lumpur without trying python soup, here's your chance. Thai Kee's Animal Soup Restaurant **(19)** offers turtle, iguana, squirrel, python, mongoose, and dog soup for between M$1.50 and M$3. In a glass showcase, there is a monkey, leopard, eagle, alligator, wildcat and a python which were eaten and stuffed.

Watch this multi-million dollar, electric car parking lot **(20)** move cars around in the air like sections of Rubic's cube. These three shops **(21)** compress an amazing number of items into a small space. They sell buttons and buckles, baskets and chinaware. On the end is a traditional Chinese trading house with its original door that allows ventilation.

To find the Sze Ya Temple **(22),** look for a dragon-studded archway next to the modern Hong Leong Finance Berhad building. The deity of the temple protected the early pioneers. Yap Ah Loy welcomed the deity in 1864 and later donated the land. You might finish the tour with lunch in the air-conditioned Futt Hup Yuen Vegetarian Restaurant **(23).**

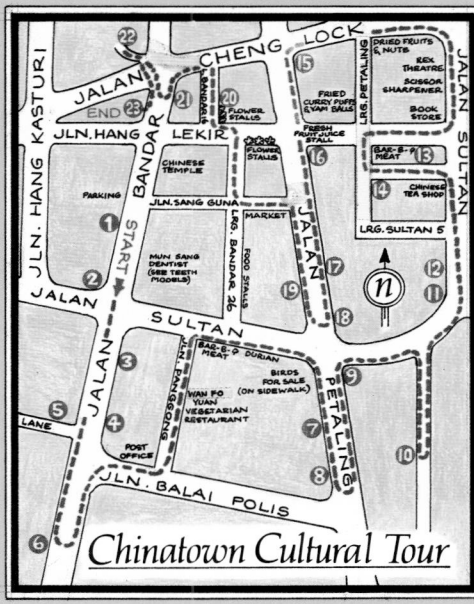

Chinatown Cultural Tour

CHINATOWN ARCHITECTURE: Resident Frank Swettenham, when he rebuilt the city in 1884, ordered covered public walkways called "five-foot ways" to provide protection from sun and rain. The shophouse, with families living above their stores, originated in southern China and was adapted to the Malaysian climate. The Selangor Chinese Assembly Hall, c. 1920 **(1)**. It took more than a decade to get this community centre built. One of the final conflicts was whether to name it after revolutionary Sun Yat Sen. The British resident threatened to hold back the land title unless the building was named the Chinese Assembly Hall and no portraits or busts of Chinese were displayed. Notice the wings above the doors and square Egyptian capitals.

The Khoon Yam Temple, **(2)** 1898 is a rather typical tile-roofed temple. Notice the archway in front that supports lions, phoenixes and dragons. The Chan See Shu Yuen Temple and Clan House, **(3)** 1906, has the best example in Malaysia of Shek Wan pottery figures from southern China, tilted slightly forward to be seen in perspective. The undulating roofline style is called "cat crawling."

Nos. 125–135 Jalan Petaling, **(4)** illustrate the development of the shophouse. Those on the left were probably built about 1900. They have floor to ceiling wooden shutters, a tropical adaptation probably borrowed from the Malay *kampung* house. The slates and balustrades at the base of the windows kept children from falling out. On each roof is another miniature roof, called a jack roof, for smoke and heat ventilation. Tiles interlock to keep out rain. The three shophouses on the right were built in the 1920s. Notice the addition of decorative columns, capitals, and cornices based on European styles then in vogue.

Nos. 18–28 Jalan Sultan **(5)**. On the first floor are three arched windows with lattice work for ventilation. The Colonial Hotel, Nos. 39–45 Jalan Sultan **(6)** is really four shophouses combined. Along the pediment are small protruding rectangles, dentils, meant to represent wooden beams. The three flame-like shapes on the roof are Greek acanthus leaves. See the courtyard and peacock tiles.

At the Yan Keng Benevolent Dramatic Association, **(7)** No. 51 Jalan Hang Jebat, notice the false roof front and the nine massive square columns. The Secondary Confucian School, **(8)**, 1922. Notice the square neo-classical columns and arch facade which form the balcony. The Selangor Grocers Guide, **(9)** No. 78 Jalan Sultan is a well preserved neo-classical building. On the two columns are smaller decorative columns sitting on pineapple bases.

Look at Nos. 9–21 Jalan Petaling **(10)** from the overpass footbridge. See the curving Dutch gable, the square ventilation slots, and the pepperpot topknots on the roof. At No. 1 Jalan Petaling, **(11)**, note the two Chinese good luck coins and fruit for long life. No. 13 Jalan Silang, **(12)**, appears to be the only shophouse in Chinatown with decorative pottery figures similar to those on the Chan Temple. At Nos. 87–89 Jalan Bandar **(13)**, c. 1914, the curly skyline is an excellent example of baroque style.

Nos. 99 and 101 Jalan Bandar, **(14)**, 1914. The building on the left has a strongly stated central pediment, like a small house perched on pineapples. The Commercial Press is the city's oldest printing company. At Nos. 14 and 16 Leboh Pasar Besar, **(15)**, look for the elaborately curved gable roof in the centre and the two columns that only support pumpkins.

Nos. 1–15 Medan Pasar **(16)**. In the 1870s, this plaza was the Market Square. The impressive shophouses on both sides of the street were built later creating an active commercial centre in the 1920s.

Gian Singh and Corner Block **(17)**, Nos. 13–21 Jalan Tun Perak, were built from 1909 to 1924 by different architects. The star and cresent in the triangular pediment indicates the owner was a Muslim. The Standard Chartered Bank **(18)**, No. 2 Jalan Benteng, 1913, features a three-storey stairway tower and was opened in 1913 as John Little's department store.

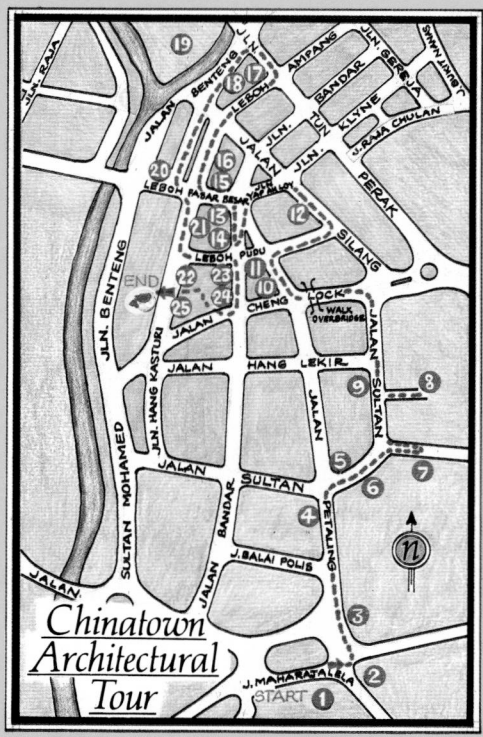

Chinatown Architectural Tour

Masjid Jame, (19), 1909, is patterned after a north Indian mosque. Nos. 2–6 Medan Pasar, (20). The four bay windows were considered an architectual feat because they left so little of the wall. Notice the Dutch step-like gables. The Vatican Bar, once a popular planters' watering hole, is housed here. No. 12 Jalan Hang Kasturi (21) has so many flowers, it appears to be growing. No. 1 Leboh Pudu (22), c. 1909. See the refined oval windows and scrolled moldings on the corner building. Nos. 113–118 Jalan Bandar (23). Notice the arched Palladian windows and large dentils. The Sze Ya Temple (24), 1883, built before the current street plan, the temple sits on a 45 degree angle to the street. Nos. 24–30 Jalan Hang Kasturi (25), are probably the best group of shophouses in the city. Notice the triangular roof pediments, "stretched" columns, the louvres and the flowers.

The Central Market (26), is a massive 1936, Art Deco building with neo-Egyptian step design on the doors, a frieze-like corregated band that runs around the structure and 22 entrances.

CHOW KIT MARKET: This is one of the two best, and largest markets in central Kuala Lumpur (the other is Pudu Market). It is open from 5 a.m. to 6 p.m. At night the produce carts roll away and the dinner carts move in and it becomes one of the most active and colourful Malay eating areas. Although you will find hawkers of all races, Chow Kit Market is known as a Malay market. It is named after Loke Chow Kit, who owned the largest department store in Kuala Lumpur at the turn of the century. The market is located at the north end of Jalan Tuanku Abdul Rahman.

Begin the tour at Cure-All Corner (1) where men spread mats on the ground with photographs of horrible diseases and offer to sell you the cure for them. You will see herbs to make your urine sweet, asthma pills guaranteed directly from General Hospital, and ivory that makes one invulnerable to acid burns. Walk down the alley to Masjid Jamek Pakistan (2), which was built in 1963. The Hoeh Beng Buddhist Temple (3), which opened in 1941, is a pleasant hidden retreat. A statue of a warrior stands outside the temple guarding a large gold statue of Lord Buddha.

Syarikat Sun Tong Tuck (4) is a Malay wedding store with elaborate imitation gold jewelry, betelnut boxes, velvet wedding bed spreads, and small baskets to hold the hard boiled eggs given to wedding guests. Photographs on the counter will give you an idea of how all the regalia is used. Kong Hock Teng Temple (5) has large green tiles with pink lotus blossoms. You will also see two tree-shaped structures lined with many small plastic windows containing miniature Buddhas. These expensive structures, imported from Taiwan, light up, revolve and play chants.

Retrace your steps and go through the eating area (6), past the chicken section. You can stop here for a drink or continue into the covered market area. Lum Hing pottery (7) sells a large variety of tea pots and bowls. Walk past the flower stalls (8) and turn right (9) to see a woman making bright red shoes, a coffee seller, a button covering shop, and a chilli maker. Walk back past the dried fish, salted eggs and spices (10) and continue past the sewing and clothes shops into the main indoor market (11) known for its quality and inexpensive fruits and vegetables. Walk to the end and through the walled-off pork section to the other half of the market (12) to see chickens, *tofu*, cockles, eggs, and rows of Indian men selling spices, including curry made to order and betelnut condiments.

Outside the covered section, walk past the herb and fish sellers (13) to a row of elevated shops (14). Walk through the outdoor market (15) and notice the *ice kacang* (snow-cones), sugared donuts, deep fried bananas, and long green *petai* beans toward the end. The Tatt Khalsa Diwan Temple (16), built in 1924, is the largest and oldest Sikh Temple in the city, according to devotees. Chappattis are cooked on Sundays over two large underground pits and served to hundreds in a large dining hall. Women must wear scarves to go in the temple. Muslim grave stones (17) are sold at this shop. The round ones are for men and flat ones for women. The Pantai Istana Ukir furniture store (18) makes elaborately carved — and heavily lacquered — furniture. You can finish the tour with lunch at Restoran Ha'adyai (19) which has excellent *tomyam* soup and barbequed chicken.

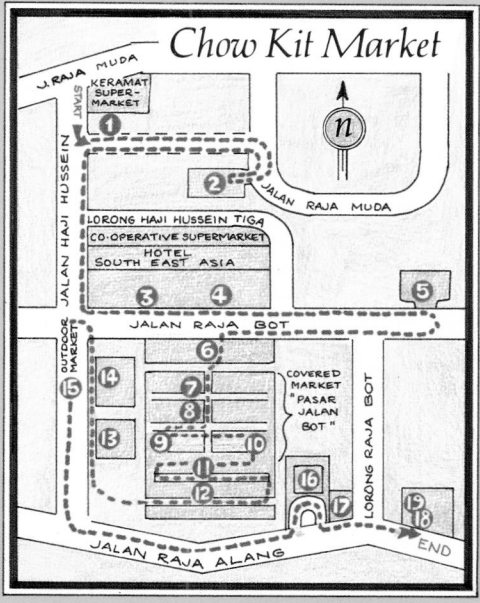

Chow Kit Market map

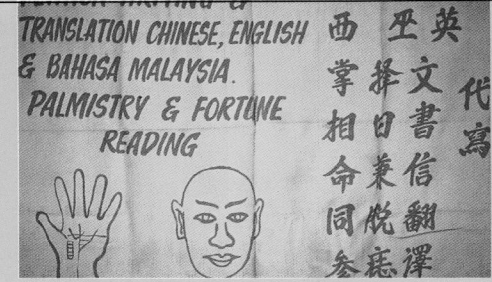

AROUND THE SHOPS: This tour includes Malay, Indian and Chinese crafts. Most of the stores are open from 9:30 a.m. to 6 p.m. and are closed Sundays. A few have set prices, but you can ask for a discount in most of the others. Start at Jalan Tuanku Abdul Rahman, formerly Batu Road, and Jalan Dang Wangi.

Selangor Pewter **(1)**, #231 Jalan Tuanku Abdul Rahman, is the largest pewter outlet in the city. Look for miniature pewter animals, pewter candlesticks, silver *kris* letter openers, pewter napkin holders, and salad servers made from Kelantan silver and buffalo horn. They will mail purchases overseas.

Peiping Lace Co. **(2)**, #223 Jalan Tuanku Abdul Rahman, has quality Chinese imports along with its sister store down the street. The store has been here 50 years and one of the owners, Goh Buck Heng, will gladly tell you the story of its name and how women wrapped themselves in lace in a bygone era. The store has mainly furniture and porcelain statues. Have a look at the air-conditioned antique jade and ivory room but be aware that prices are up to one-third more here than in duty free ports because of import taxes. Syarikat China Arts **(3)**, 219 Jalan Tuanku Abdul Rahman, has cloisonne jewellery and a variety of gift items, but some are of lesser quality. Peiping Lace Co. **(4)**, 217 Jalan Tuanku Abdul Rahman, stocks lacey nightgowns, silk blouses, embroidered table cloths, Thai blue and white pottery, and colourful Chinese jackets. They sell small gold-thread embroidered tapestries, ranging from M$18–$40, that can be framed or sewn on pillows. They also mail purchases overseas.

Sarong and Dress Stalls **(5)**, Lorong Bunus Enam, are a good place to buy *sarongs* — plaid for men, patterns for women — and have the seam sewed on the spot for M$1. The long cotton Indonesian dresses here cost M$10 — do bargain — and are ideal for the climate. If you prefer to try one on in privacy, they are also sold at the Mun Loong department store a block away. Madras Store **(6)**, 102 Jalan Masjid India, sells punjabi suits, *saris*, glass bracelets, but no *madras* material. They have M$1,000 wedding *saris* made with gold thread, and will gladly show you how to wrap six yards around you and keep it all on.

Kwality Arts **(7)**, 70A Jalan Masjid India, is owned by Niranjan Singh who claims to be one of the city's largest importers of brass and wood crafts from India. Don't let his postage stamp sized store fool you. He has a warehouse with more stock and his daughter has a store nearby. If you want to send something overseas, he can get you the best price by having it sent directly from India to your home country.

If you need some refreshment at this point, stop at Jothy's Restaurant for good north Indian food or go to Zam Zam Restoran for *roti canai* and fresh lime juice. Toko Batik Indonesia **(8)**, 2004 Masjid India, sells Indonesian shirts, material and *sarongs*. Aked Ibu

Kota **(9)**, 41–43 Jalan Tuanku Abdul Rahman (directly behind the mosque) is a narrow alley crammed with *sarongs*, embroidered bed sheets, and framed Koran verses. The Malay Clothes Arcade **(10)**, is a row of Malay shops elevated from the street. Malays come here to rent traditional clothes for important ceremonial occasions — such as being named a *datuk.* You will also see betelnut boxes, embroidered fans, shawls, black *songkoks* and ornamental tiaras. Take a look at the boxes of Jamu, Indonesia concoctions to improve one's sexual life.

Batek Malaysia Berhad **(11)**, 9 Jalan Tun Perak, is the largest *batik* store in Kuala Lumpur. Cross Tun Perak and catch a taxi going toward Jalan Raja Chulan and follow this road east to the government Karyaneka Handicraft Centre near Wisma Stephens. This has individual cottages for crafts from each state but the only two you might want to visit are Sabah and Sarawak. Otherwise go to the main centre which has brown and black pots — some say these are too fragile to mail — gold embroidered velvet purses, gold and silver threaded material, *songkets,* and sometimes an interesting weaving demonstration. Relax in the International Crafts Museum garden.

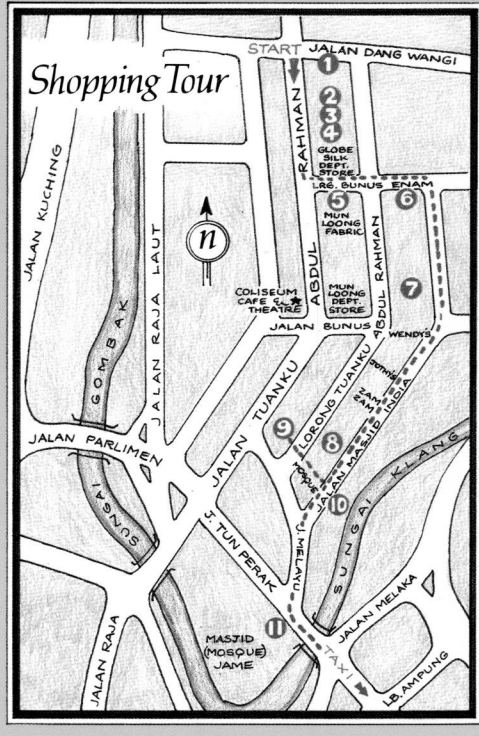

Off the Beaten Track

KAMPUNG AMPANG, an old Hakka tin mining village, has a peaceful stream, a medicine temple and excellent *tofu*, called *tau foo* locally. Take Jalan Ampang west into the town and stop at the small Boh Tea packing plant. Then take Jalan Lembah Jaya that leads to the Ampang stream where people wash motorcycles, shampoo their hair and swim. Take a jungle walk, but watch out for leeches. Back in the village visit the Tham Kong Temple, built in 1938, to learn how devotees looking for cures once tossed sticks to see what medication the deity recommended. Then have a mixed *yeung tau foo* (stuffed bean curd) lunch at the locally famed — but simple — Kedai Makanan Foong Foong, closed Mondays.

THE HOLY TOMB, OR *KERAMAT*, AT KAMPUNG DATUK KERAMAT was established by the government in the 1960s. West of the market is a shrine to a couple known only as the old Java man and the old Java woman. The couple were a well-known part of the area in the early 1900s. When the man died, it is said he contacted his wife through her dreams. Soon she became a medium for people wanting to know the future or speak to the dead. When she died they were buried together in this shrine. Today, the shrine still appeals to people of all faiths who come here to ask for favours or guidance. At the front of the building are some small graves, reputed to belong to babies killed in World War II. To reach the market, go west on Jalan Ampang, turn left at Jalan Jelatik, and then left on Jalan Keramat Dalam.

THE BATHROOMS AT LE COQ D'OR RESTAURANT. The men's bathroom on the ground floor has designer urinals, decorative tiles, and an opium couch inlaid with marble, with plenty of room for paraphernalia to create opium dreams. In the women's bathroom and dressing room, it may be necessary to step over the sleeping servants and past a sign that says "Do not pass water on the floor" in English and Chinese. Do not disturb the man who lives on the balcony around to the back.

TWO CHINESE MANSIONS that were once the most magnificent homes in the city. Loke Hall, built in 1907, is just off Jalan Parlimen behind Bank Rakyat. It was built by an early mining and department store magnate, Loke Chow Kit, for his home and mining offices. The occupants, the Malaysian Institute of Architects, invite tourists to look around and buy their publications, including the helpful *Guide to Kuala Lumpur Notable Buildings*. Loke Chow Kit's good friend, Loke Yew, lived not far away on Medan Tuanku off Jalan Tuanku Abdul Rahman. Loke Yew, one of the first multimillionaires in Malaysia, built Wisma Loke in 1904. The house was surrounded by 11 acres of palms and was the first in the city to be lit by electricity. It has both Renaissance and Chinese influences — see the round moon door — and was used

as a Japanese headquarters in World War II. The building was vacant in early 1986 and it is not known who the new tenants will be.

BUKIT NANAS, named Pineapple Hill after a plantation that used to exist there, is a pleasant historical walk. Begin at Jalan Raja Chulan. Here, a Dutch mercenary fought to save Kuala Lumpur in the Selangor Civil War in 1872 and lost. The hill is notable for its gothic and neoclassical Catholic schools and churches — St. John's Cathedral, 1955, St. John's Institution, 1907, and the Convent of the Holy Infant Jesus, 1912. When St. John's Institution was being built, tigers sometimes attacked the oxen that carried supplies. Today, one can sometimes hear students practice bagpipes on the school field in the afternoon.

THE GUINNESS BREWERY has the latest non-alcoholic soft drink, called Malta. Malaysia was the first country in Southeast Asia to test-market the drink, because it appears to fit Malaysian tastes for things spicy, salty and sweet — at the same time. To tour the plant, a half hour south on the Federal Highway, write P.O. Box 144, Petaling Jaya or call the public relations officer at 776–3022. After the 45-minute tour, you are served free beer and snacks.

BIRD-SINGING CONTESTS are held monthly in several different locations. Birds are pulled up seven-metre poles and judged on various aspects of their performance. The bird accessories on sale are as interesting as the competition. To find out about the next event, call the bird store Syrikat Cheong Heng at 783–6361 or other bird stores.

FOR A NIGHT OUT. Try the Petaling Street night market and a movie at the Rex Theatre on Jalan Sultan. Arrive about an hour and a half before the show and walk down Jalan Hang Lekir and Jalan Petaling. These streets are alive at night with snake oil salesmen, steamboat and clay-pot chicken rice stalls, and plastic jewellery salesmen. Have dinner at a stall. You can't go wrong with *mee sup*, noodle soup, or *nasi goreng*, fried rice — and then take in a movie. The advertisements at the beginning are fun. Under Malaysian law, it's illegal to show any human element in a cigarette ad. So watch for dancing cigarettes.

A DOUBLE SCOOP OF VANILLA ICE CREAM in a cocktail glass with Tia Maria liqueur at the Coliseum Cafe on a weekend night, when the bar is crowded with Indians and Chinese who are arguing about the meaning of life and other topics.

TRY JUNGLE-BASHING, an old sport originally practised by the colonials and described today as a "test of strength." It's easy. About eight people go into the jungle with *parangs*, or large knives, and cut their way through. Then they retreat to where they started — or to the nearest source of cold beer. There is plenty of jungle, but make sure you have permission and can find your way out.

SOUTHEAST ASIA'S BEST COMPREHEN-SIVE COLLECTION OF CERAMICS at the Muzium Seni Asia, or Museum of Asian Art at the University of Malaya campus. This museum also has a collection of "capings," or modesty discs to cover the private parts of small boys as well as girls, and other interesting Asian artifacts.

DRIVE THROUGH KENNY HILLS, the city's most exclusive and beautiful suburb, now called Bukit Tunku. The Wp.1 map of Kuala Lumpur is very handy for this trip. Drive up Jalan Kuching to Jalan Duta and turn left at the government complex roundabout. Explore Jalan Syers and its old colonial houses, and Jalan Tunku, where you can feed the monkeys and see the modest home of Tunku Abdul Rahman, the father of modern Malaysia, at the very south end of Jalan Tunku. Drive back to the Duta roundabout and continue on to Jalan Duta, to the new suburb of Taman Duta, where you will find a seven-storey castle named Camelot at #10 Cangkat Duta. Around the corner at #2 Lorong Duta Lima is one of Malaysia's finest homes, commonly called the White House, built by businessman-politician Tan Koon Swan, elected head of the Malaysian Chinese Association in 1985.

THE MALAYSIAN ORCHID NURSERY near Subang Airport has 300 types of orchids, in all 100,000 potted orchids covering two hectares. They sell both cut and potted orchids and will package them for air travel. Some flower shops will mail cut orchids overseas, but it is quite costly. The nursery is on the right on the way to the airport about 20 km. from town. It is open seven days a week, from 7 a.m. to 7 p.m. The telephone number is 776-7016.

MALAYSIA'S LARGEST AND MOST ELABORATE CHINESE TEMPLE is also its newest. Take the Federal Highway to Jalan Robson, then go to Pesiaran Endah and the Thean Hou Temple. Built by the Hainanese community, this M$10 million temple honours the Goddess of the Sea with a 3 metre statue. The domed ceiling contains 700-odd protruding figures of the goddess. There is a three-tiered roof, complete with phoenix and dragon sculptures. The temple also has an excellent view of Kuala Lumpur.

CAREY ISLAND, Pulau Carey, near Klang (also spelled Kelang) has wood carvings by the Mah-Meri aborigines. Sculptures and masks, ranging in price from around M$100 to M$300, represent different spirits that are explained in a brochure by the National Museum. On the island, you will drive through a Harrisons & Crosfield oil palm estate and visit the village, but most of the aborigines, or Orang Asli, are away during the day so don't expect to see carving or much community life. It takes three months to have a specific sculpture made. To make group arrangements, call the Aborigines Department, 559-0375. Eat at the restaurant at the island bridge.

THE GEDUNG RAJA ABDULLAH MUSEUM in Klang, just over the Klang River, is a former tin storehouse and residence which was recently restored and opened. The building played a prominent role in the Selangor Civil War in the 1860s. Walk around the area to see other historic government buildings and some interesting pawn shops. For lunch, try the Port View Restaurant at the wharf in nearby Port Klang for seafood and a view of the boats of the Straits of Malacca. You can hire a boat to tour the port.

HORSE RACING at the Selangor Turf Club on Jalan Ampang can be watched on Saturday and Sunday at 2 p.m. — when the horses are running. Live racing is rotated among several tracks around the country and Singapore. To find out racing days, call 243-3077. When the horses are at other tracks, off-track betting takes place at the Sungei Besi centre, 12 km. south on the Seremban highway.

THE CITY'S LARGEST CEMETERY has two tombstone carving shops, two crematoriums and one of the largest Chinese temples in the city. The cemetery is on Jalan Kerayong south of Edinburgh round-about. Farther up the road is a crematorium and the Chin Foot Sze Temple, often called the Thousand Buddha Temple because of the many tiles with the image of Lord Buddha. The temple was restored in 1985, but in the rear there are still old doors made without metal hinges and three graphic paintings de-picting punishments in Hell for prostitution and murder. A similar painting is located at the Khoon Yam Temple, 161 Jalan Ampang.

DRIVE UP BUKIT GASING, or Gasing Hill, to get an impressive view of Kuala Lumpur and Petaling Jaya. Look for the many tin mine lakes — some mines still function — and you can get an idea of the role played by tin in the area's early history. Take the Federal Highway to Jalan Gasing and drive to Jalan 5/64, which takes you up to the Sivan Temple at the top of the hill. Then visit the nearby Chetawan Temple, 24 Jalan Pantai, an impressive Thai Buddhist temple that was recently renovated.

FOR A SHORT DRIVE INTO DENSE JUNGLE — the way all Malaysia once appeared — visit Janda Baik, a small village with a pleasant wading stream about 45 minutes from Kuala Lumpur. Take the Kuantan highway northeast, to the turnoff for the Genting Highlands gambling resort. Take that turnoff, then turn left another 200-odd metres up the road. Follow it a few kilometres to the town.

THE FOREST RESEARCH INSTITUTE, open-ed to the public in late 1986, offers a waterfall and tours of plant life. Call 626-2633. It is located in Kepong, about 40 minutes from Kuala Lumpur.

BANDAR, the old temporary royal capital of Selangor, is about an hour and a half from Kuala Lumpur in the Kuala Langat district south of Klang.

First take a detour into Morib to see the modern palace of the sultan and visit the beach where a monument stands to Lord Louis Mountbatten's Southeast Asian Command, which landed troops and vehicles here at the end of WWII. In the Bandar area, visit the royal mausoleum of Sultan Abdul Samad, sultan of Selangor during Kuala Lumpur's early years. Farther up the road is an old charcoal factory with towering ovens, which burn mangrove wood. You can get clay-baked beggar's chicken, but it must be ordered a day ahead. The *istana*, or palace, in Bandar was originally built only as a retreat by his Royal Highness Tengku Sulaiman, at the turn of the century. Later, he moved there from the official *istana* in Klang because of a dispute with his consort. But two years later, he returned to Klang and the temporary palace fell into disrepair. It is still unsafe to enter. Next to it is an impressive mosque and nearby, a river.

TAKE A COUNTRY DRIVE through rubber and oil palm estates to Kuala Selangor and its historic forts and lighthouse and a neighbouring fishing village, an hour north on the coast. Fort Altingsburg on Bukit Melawati was held by the Dutch for a year before they were routed by the Malays in 1785. Despite the fact this and another nearby fort have been in Malay hands for two centuries, both have kept their Dutch names. A rest house, which serves curry tiffin lunch, is also on the hill, along with a colony of monkeys.

WATCH THE TRANSVESTITES, or *pondans*, ply their trade beside the Selangor Club after 10 p.m.

GAMBLE AT GENTING HIGHLANDS Complex, the only casino in the country. Tour buses leave the major hotels daily for the hour journey to the 2,000 metre hill station. The resort includes an artificial lake with boats, a miniature railway for children, a golf course, a bowling alley, and a new cave temple. Although not considered a top quality resort by many, it does offer lots of instant entertainment.

MARKETS. Walk through a day or night market to put your finger on the pulse of Kuala Lumpur. The two best day "wet" markets in the city are Pudu and Chow Kit. At night, Petaling Street closes for inexpensive clothing and jewelry stalls and food hawkers. Chow Kit also comes alive at night with roll-away food carts. A Malay market has been set up on Tuanku Abdul Rahman on Saturday nights for crafts, herbal cures and Malay food. In the old Malay settlement of Kampung Baru, there is a Saturday night market, called the Sunday Market, with cluttered curio and handicraft stores.

WATCH POISONOUS SCORPIONS fight it out at your feet at the city's bug preserving centre. Syarikat Papillon makes plastic paperweights, penholders and keychains containing scorpions, butterflies and other creatures to be shipped around the world. The factory has 100,000 scorpions, beetles, spiders, butterflies and other insects — mostly gathered by the Orang Asli, or aborigines, who catch the insects in the jungle. There is a pen of live scorpions at the entrance. It is located near Batu Caves by the Kuantan highway and is a bit difficult to find (Phone 689–2000).

CRAB ISLAND, or Pulau Ketam, is a Chinese fishing community of about 11,200 people living in houses on stilts over a mudflat island near Port Klang. The village relies on rain water for washing, and food — other than fish — comes from the mainland. This is a full day's trip. Leave Kuala Lumpur about 8:15 a.m. and take the Federal Highway to Port Klang, about an hour's drive. Drive straight to the port at the end of the road, park and walk to the end of the pier. Here you board a sampan for 40 *sen* that will take you a short distance to the ferry, which leaves about 9:30 a.m. Boats run every hour. The boatman rows standing up in traditional Chinese fashion. The ferry is M$2. When you reach the community, you switch to a smaller boat for a 30 *sen* ride to the shore. The town has restaurants, temples, schools, boat repair shops, clinics and a theatre. The ferries leave every hour. To avoid Federal Highway rush hour traffic going back into Kuala Lumpur, leave by 2:30 p.m.

VISIT THE LUSH COUNTRYSIDE around Kuala Lumpur to see a rattan shop, the country's most innovative *batik* factory, and to buy flowers at the Sungai Buloh leprosarium — all in half a day. Take Jalan Duta to the suburb of Bukit Damansara. Go through the suburb to Jalan Damansara. Nine miles from Kuala Lumpur on Jalan Damansara is Bumikraft Sdn. Bhd. This is a small rattan shop that makes furniture. The store is open Monday through Saturday. A short distance up the road on the right is a sign for Kutang Kraft. Follow this small road about one km. through rubber trees to Kampung Sungei Penchala. The village next to the *batik* factory is the home of a conservative Islamic sect so expect to see veiled women. At the Kutang Kraft showroom you will find cotton, voile, silk and jersey *batiks*. But before you buy a *sarong* or a piece to be framed, walk down into the factory. If you see a pattern you like, ask for a similar one or design one yourself. Open Monday through Saturday.

Continue up Jalan Damansara to the "T" intersection at Jalan Sungei Buloh and turn left. Drive 4.7 km. until you see the sign for the National Leprosy Control Centre, (Pusat Kawalan Kusta Negara, Sungai Buloh). Take the road to the right that goes over a railroad track to the entrance. You can buy plants and cut flowers for very reasonable prices at any of the small nurseries in front of the chalets. The disease is not contagious once treated — which is evident from the crowds who come here.

GO JOGGING in Lake Gardens (Taman Tasek Perdana) on Sime Darby Bhd.'s new Parcourse, which includes outdoor exercise equipment.

K.L. Best Bets

SUNNY POOLSIDE LUNCH at the Hilton Hotel, Jalan Sultan Ismail, for Italian food, a view of the race track and a pleasant time watching bathers.

JAZZ AT ALL THAT JAZZ, 14 Jalan 19/36, Petaling Jaya (755–3152).

TRADITIONAL MASSAGE by blind masseurs at the Professional Blind Service Centre, 4A Jalan Thambapillai, Brickfields (274–1337). You can request a male or female masseur.

EAR CLEANING and $4 haircut at outdoor barber on the Muttiah Chetty Lane off Jalan Sultan, Chinatown.

MALAY ANTIQUES at H. Raby Antiques, No. 3, Pinggiran Ukay, Jalan Ulu Klang (457–3698). (Don't expect antique bargains in Malaysia — dealers know the value of their goods. But don't hestitate to negotiate.)

MALACCA FURNITURE at La Dame De Malacca, 11 Jalan Pinang, next to Holiday Inn (248–4709).

SOUTHEAST ASIAN SOUVENIRS at Man Art Gallery, Hilton Hotel (243–1724) and Star Gems & Gifts, Yow Chuan Plaza (248–0019) and at Ampang Park (248–3173). Ask for a discount.

NEW ROSEWOOD FURNITURE at Kok Art and Craft, 12, Jalan Bandar 3, Taman Melawati, Setapak (407–2548) or Peiping Lace Co., 223 Jalan Tuanku Abdul Rahman (298–3184).

CHINESE CRAFTS at Peiping Lace Co. (their second store), 217 Jalan Tuanku Abdul Rahman (292–9282) and next door at Syarikat China Arts, 219 Jalan Tuanku Abdul Rahman (292–9250).

MALAY CRAFTS at Karyaneka Handicraft Centre, 186 Jalan Raja Chulan, open every day (241–3704).

MOST INNOVATIVE, COLOURFUL BATIK is at the Kutang Kraft factory at Kampung Sungei Penchala, about 16 km. from Kuala Lumpur.

SELECTION OF PEWTER at Selangor Pewter showroom, 231 Jalan Tuanku Abdul Rahman (298–6244).

CHILDREN'S ENTERTAINMENT at Mimaland, 18 km. from the city. It is a large park with boating, fishing, games, and a giant swimming pool with water slides. Park and pool entrance fees are M$4. For shopping centre amusement parks, children enjoy Asiajaya's Family Fun World, opposite the Petaling Jaya Hilton.

ALL-ROUND SHOPPING COMPLEX is Sungei Wang Plaza and Bukit Bintang Plaza (both in one building) at corner of Jalan Sultan Ismail and Jalan Bukit Bintang. Although a confusing jumble of stores, this centre does have large upscale department stores — Klasse, Metrojaya and City Chemist — for most needs. This is also the best place to see modern Malaysia in action — whole families come here for evening outings. The best modern shopping centre is KL Plaza a block away.

BOOKSTORE is Berita Book Centre, first floor, Bukit Bintang Plaza or, farther out of town, the University of Malaya Bookstore has a wide selection and low prices.

TRAVEL BOOK for practical information outside of Kuala Lumpur is *Malaysia, Singapore & Brunei, A Travel Survival Kit* by Lonely Planet Publications.

HISTORICAL AND COLOURFUL BOOKS on Malaysia are *Noone of the Ulu* by Dennis Holman; *The Soul of Malaya* by Henri Fauconnier; *The Golden Chersonese: Travels in Malaya in 1879* by Isabella Bird; *Malay Sketches* by Sir Frank Swettenham; *The Jungle is Neutral* by F. Spencer Chapman; *Taman Budiman: Memoirs of an Unorthodox Civil Servant* by Tan Sri Dato Mubin Sheppard; *The Story of Kuala Lumpur (1857–1939)* by J.M. Gullick; *Malaya 1948–1960: The War of the Running Dogs* by Noel Barber; and *The Long Day Wanes: A Malayan Trilogy* by Anthony Burgess.

PLACE TO FIND UPCOMING EVENTS AND ENTERTAINMENT is the Metropolis section of *The Star* newspaper and best classified ads are in *The Malay Mail*.

VIEWS OF KUALA LUMPUR are from: **City Hall,** Jalan Raja Laut, 29th floor balcony. A security guard will escort you during working hours, but guards request tourists be modestly dressed — no shorts or halter tops. **Dayabumi Complex,** Jalan Raja, has organized tours of the building and roof helicopter pad on Sat. 9:30 a.m. and 2:30 p.m., Sun. 9:30 a.m. (274–8899). The **Hilton Hotel's** Paddock restaurant on the 30th floor has a splendid view of the racetrack and surroundings.

DISCOS are the Tin Mine Discotheque, Hilton Hotel, a favourite escape for royalty and jet setters, the Sapphire disco at Yow Chuan Plaza and Hollywood East at Ampang Park.

PUB is Rogues Gallery Restoran, 19 Jalan 521/1, Petaling Jaya (757–0863), near the PJ Hilton and MPPJ building. **Most homey bar** is the "library" at The Suasa Brasserie, Regent Hotel — but it is wise to ask the price before ordering.

HAIRSTYLING at Michael Choi, Bangunan Angkasa Raya, Jalan Ampang (242–5150). For medium price, try A Cut Above, T19–20 KL Plaza, Jalan Bukit Bintang (242–5956). For a good haircut, manicure and pedicure all for under M$20 try Winnie Unisex Salon, 4A Lorong Kolam Air Lama 1, Ampang Jaya (456–0631).

MEN'S TAILOR is Jim's Shop in Jaya Supermarket, Petaling Jaya (757–5620).

DRESSMAKER for western styles is Ann's Feysen, 2–B Lorong Kolam Air Lama 1, Ampang Jaya (456–4824). She also makes traditional Malay dresses — *baju kurong* and *baju kebaya* — with a modern flair.

JUNGLE AND BIRD SOUNDS are from the Malayan Nature Society, PO Box 10750, KL (775–3330). The three tapes include "Voices of the Forest," used in the Tarzan movie "Greystoke".

MALACCA AND PENANG NYONYA FOOD at Nyonya Restoran, 52 Jalan SS 2/24, SEA Park, Petaling Jaya (775–9709) or Sri Ampang Restoran, 32A Pesiaran Ampang (456–4526). Sri Ampang also has a dessert to write home about — fried ice cream.

STEAK at Jake's Charbroiled Steaks, 21A Jalan Setiapuspa (254–5677) or closer to town, Castell Pub & Grill or The Ship.

INDIAN FOOD at Ala'din Restaurant, lower ground 14, Wilayah Shopping Centre (292–6805) or Shiraz Restaurant, 1 Jalan Medan Tuanku (292–0159). Best Indian banana leaf at Raju Restaurant, 27 Jalan 5/13, Petaling Jaya (756–1361) or closer to town, Bilal Restaurant, 33 Jalan Ampang (238–0804).

MALAY FOOD at Indah 'Ku, third floor, Kuwasa Building, Jalan Raja Laut (293–1372) or Yazmin, second floor, Ampang Park (248–7377). Both serve buffets and have a Malay cultural dance show.

JUNGLE WALK is the very old 11-hectare Bukit Nanas Forest Reserve, with labelled trees, a fruit display, timber museum and monkeys.

THAI FOOD at Sri Siam Restaurant, 58 Jalan SS 2/24, Petaling Jaya (775–3076) or for very elegant surroundings try Chao Phaya Seafood Restaurant, OUG Plaza, Jalan Klang Lama (782–7167).

FOOD STALLS are the Munshi Abdullah covered stalls behind Campbell Shopping Kompleks on Jalan Dang Wangi and the Campbell stalls that fill the nearby parking lot at night. Or in Petaling Jaya go to Medan Selera next to Jaya Supermarket, Section 14, 14/20, or Taman Selera, Section 1, Old Town.

DIM SUM at Mandarin Garden Restaurant, Federal Hotel, 35 Jalan Bukit Bintang (248–9166), open Sun. and holidays from 8 a.m.–2:30 p.m., on other days from 12–2:30 p.m. For those on a small budget, there is very good dim sum at Kedai Makanan Yoke Woo Him, 100 Petaling Street, from 6 a.m. daily.

CONTINENTAL FOOD for big budgets at Restaurant Lafite, Shangri-La Hotel (232–2388) and for medium budgets at The Suasa Brasserie, Regent Hotel (243–2284).

CHINESE FOOD:
—Big budget: Happy Valley Seafood & Sharkfin Restaurant, Menara Promet, Jalan Sultan Ismail (241–1264).
—Medium budget: Golden Phoenix Restaurant, Hotel Equatorial, Jalan Sultan Ismail (261–3608).
—For clay-baked beggar's chicken or duck: Overseas Restoran, 86 Jalan Imbi (248–7567). Order by 10 a.m. for dinner.
—For Hakka food: Hakka Restaurant, Chin Woo Athletic Assn., off Jalan Hang Jebat (238–1069). Try

black pork or steamboat while the sun goes down and watch the swimmers and *tai chi* performers at the Chin Woo Stadium pool, which overlooks the city skyline, and is open to the public.
—For pleasant atmosphere, try The Pines and other Chinese open-air restaurants on Jalan Tun Sambanthan in Brickfields.

CLUBS TO JOIN — even if you are here only a short time — are the Malayan Nature Society (775–3330); Malaysian Culture Group (248–7293); and Friends of the Heritage of Malaysia Society, 4–6 Jalan Tangsi, KL. The Nature Society has photography, bird watching and caving groups.

PRACTICAL BOOK for people moving to Kuala Lumpur is *Selamat Datang* by the American Association (293–4733).

CANE FURNITURE at McGuiree Cane Trading, Lot 1, Pinggiram Ukay, Ulu Klang (457–5696).

PRIVATE ART GALLERIES are: On-Tai Gallery, a non-profit gallery and the city's largest at Wisma On-Tai, Jalan Ampang (261–4122). Farther out of town is Saujana Fine Arts Gallery, 51 Jalan SS 15/4, Subang Jaya (734–1476). Rupa Design, 15 Jalan 8/7, Petaling Jaya, (755–9142) is small but specialises in pictures of Malaysia's architectural heritage. The owner is Victor Chin, a leader in preserving historical buildings.

COLONIAL RESTAURANTS for reminiscing about British rule are the Coliseum Cafe, 98 Jalan Tuanku Abdul Rahman (292–6270) and Le Coq d'Or, 121 Jalan Ampang (242–9732). They are considered Kuala Lumpur institutions and a must.

TOURIST MAP of Kuala Lumpur is Lani's Kuala Lumpur Discovery Map which shows historic buildings, markets, temples, and places to eat, available at Berita bookstores and the Kuala Lumpur Visitors Centre (230–1369).

WEEKLY POLITICAL NEWSPAPER COLUMNS are "As I See It" by former Prime Minister Tunku Abdul Rahman and "Without Fear or Favour" by Tan Sri Dr. Tan Chee Koon, both in *The Star*.

CONVERSATION PIECE is a coconut scraper — your friends will never guess what it is. Antique wooden ones with carved animals or boys for seats sell for M$300 and more, but modern ones sell for M$6 at market kitchen shops.

CAVES are Batu Caves, possibly 120 million years old, home to aborigines, tigers and bears before becoming a Hindu temple in 1891. Japanese murdered nearly 40 communists here in 1942, betrayed by a triple agent. A cave art gallery has colourful statues and nearby sacred five-and-six-legged cows munch grass.

INEXPENSIVE AND MODEST COTTON DRESSES to combat tropical weather are found at Mun Loong department store, 113 Jalan Tuanku Abdul Rahman, or at outside stalls up the block at Lorong Bunus Enam. Price: about M$10.

Family boats motor up inlets at Crab Island, two hours from Kuala Lumpur. The community — living in houses on stilts over the water — provides schooling for 1,150 students and has a boat repair factory, temples and clinics.

Travel Notes

Land and People

Peninsular Malaysia is located in the central part of Southeast Asia between latitudes 1 degree and 7 degrees north and longitudes 100 degrees and 105 degrees east. To the north are Burma, Thailand, Laos, Kampuchea and Vietnam. To the south are Singapore and Indonesia.

The country is comprised of the Malay Peninsula and the states of Sabah and Sarawak on Borneo island. It has a multi-racial population of about 15.7 million including Malays, Chinese, Indians and the indigenous people of Sabah and Sarawak. The country is governed by a parliamentary democracy with a constitutional monarch. Kuala Lumpur, often called K.L., is the federal capital. It covers an area of 244 sq km. and has a population of under one million.

How to Get There

By Air:
More than 20 airlines serve Malaysia from around the world. Kuala Lumpur's Subang International Airport is a very modern facility 22 km. from the city centre. It links with 12 major domestic airports. Malaysia's airline, Malaysian Airline System (MAS), operates domestic flights to Sabah, Sarawak, Penang, east coast cities on the peninsula and other locations. An airline with smaller planes, MACAIR, goes to airports at Langkawi, Malacca and Tioman Island. Kuala Lumpur is 40 minutes from Singapore and an hour and 20 minutes from Bangkok.

By Rail:
There is an express train from Bangkok to Kuala Lumpur three times a week. It is a two-day trip and sleeping berths are available. The train also goes from Singapore to Kuala Lumpur six times a day and the trip takes 6½ hours, with sleepers available. There is a 10-day railpass available but it is not very economical because of the limited rail lines in Malaysia.

By Bus:
Express buses from Singapore to Kuala Lumpur run regularly and cost about M$20.

Weather

It is hot, humid and sunny all year round. The temperature is usually between 21° and 32°C and the average rainfall is between 2,000 and 2,500 mm. Monsoons hit the east coast of Peninsular Malaysia and Sabah and Sarawak from October to February. This is not a good time to visit the east coast, where the best beaches are, although hotels are cheaper and sometimes the weather is sunny. The rainy season in the west coast is much lighter and comes from September to December. It should not deter travellers.

Customs and Entry Rules

The penalty for trafficking in illegal drugs is death. Malaysia has executed a number of people under this no-nonsense ruling.

United States citizens do not need visas for business or social visits or student study programs, but they need visas for employment in the country. Those who do not need a visa are Commonwealth citizens, British protected persons, citizens of the Republic of Ireland, Switzerland and the Netherlands.

Those who do not need visas for visits up to three months are citizens of Austria, Belgium, Denmark, Finland, France, Iceland, Italy, Japan, Luxembourg, Norway, South Korea, Sweden, Tunisia and West Germany. Citizens of ASEAN countries do not need visas for one-month visits.

There is no duty on personal effects — items the tourist needs for personal use during the journey. You can also bring in cameras, pocket calculators, video tapes, and some other items without paying duty. There is a 50 per cent duty charged on a long list of items including tape decks, carpets, typewriters, televisions, and leather handbags. But visitors can bring in duty free gifts and souvenirs that are valued at M$200 (US$80) or less. Also visitors coming to Malaysia for at least 72 hours can bring in duty free one litre of spirits, 200 cigarettes, cosmetics valued up to M$200, some clothes, electric appliances for personal care, and other items. For more detailed rules ask for the booklet "Your Malaysian Customs Regulations Guide." Visitors who do not have any dutiable goods can go through the green line without being inspected, others go through the red line.

Airport Information

MAS has a baggage office where you can leave luggage for 24 hours for M$2 per piece. The airport has prayer rooms for Muslims and an excellent nursery centre for mothers. In the arrival hall, there are toll-free telephone booths for local calls. At the departure level there are booths for international calls and a telegraph office. A Tourist Information Centre is open from 8:10 a.m.–11:30 p.m. (775–5707).

To take a taxi into town, you must buy a ticket from a counter outside the arrival hall. All prices are set. No tipping is needed, no matter how much luggage you are carrying with you. It is about M$17 to downtown.

An airport tax is collected for departing passengers: M$3 for domestic flights, M$5 for Singapore and Brunei, and M$15 for other international flights.

Health

There are no cholera or smallpox vaccinations required. Yellow fever vaccinations are required for those coming from infected areas except for children

under one year of age. Malaria pills are not needed in Kuala Lumpur, but some doctors recommend taking them when visiting rural areas. Malaria and dengue fever, sometimes called bone-break fever and also spread by mosquitoes, are small but persistent problems outside the city.

Health standards in Malaysia are among the highest in Southeast Asia. Tap water is safe to drink, although some residents boil their water to rid it of the chlorine taste and filter it.

Most foreigners prefer to use the medical facilities at Pantai Medical Centre (757–5077) and Assunta Hospital (792–3433) to the government General Hospital (292–1044). The University Hospital (756–4422) has also been recently upgraded, but they often do not answer the telephone. All three hospitals have 24-hour emergency departments.

Pets need health certificates from the country of origin. There is no quarantine for animals from Australia, New Zealand, Brunei, Singapore or the United Kingdom. But pets from other countries require a one-month quarantine. Malaysia itself is basically free of rabies.

What to Wear

Wear light cottons, but remember this is largely a Muslim country and women should not wear sleeveless tops or shorts. For most social occasions men are expected to wear *batik* shirts, rather than a suit and tie. Although it cools down at night, sweaters are generally not needed. You don't need a raincoat either, just buy an umbrella when you get here. Hotel charges for laundry are high.

Money

There are two banks exchanging money at Subang International Airport. The currency is the Malaysian *ringgit*, also called a dollar, which is divided into 100 *sen* or cents. Notes are $1, $5, $10, $20, $50, $100, $500, and $1,000.

Banks are generally open from 10 a.m.–3 p.m. Monday through Friday and from 9:30–11:30 a.m. on Saturday. Money changers are open for longer hours, often give fairly good rates for cash, and take traveller's cheques. The banks offer the best rate for traveller's cheques, but often there is a long wait. Major hotels give an inferior rate. American Express, Diners Club and other credit cards are accepted at major stores and restaurants.

Tipping

There is little tipping in Malaysia. Most hotels and restaurants add a 10 per cent service charge, in addition to a 5 per cent government tax, to the bill so tipping is not needed. Tipping is not customary at food stalls or with taxi drivers. If you visit a temple, it is polite — but not necessary — to leave a small donation, possibly 50 *sen* to M$1.

Bargaining

You should bargain — or if that makes you uncomfortable, simply ask for a discount — at most stores except for large department stores. Even stores in modern shopping complexes will drop their prices. You can usually get from 5 to 15 per cent off the price, including items such as clothes and film. If the item is not tagged, then certainly bargain. There is no discount on books. Night markets are notorious for hiking prices up by as much as 50 per cent.

Taxis

Taxis charge 70 *sen* for the first mile or 1.6 km. and 30 *sen* for each additional half mile or 0.8 km. An extra 20 per cent is added for air-conditioned cars, and may go up to 30 per cent. From 1 a.m. to 6 a.m. there is an additional 50 per cent charge above the normal rate.

You can wave a taxi down anywhere but be aware that some Malaysians think there is nothing wrong with standing farther up the street to get the taxi first. You tell the taxi driver where you want to go and he decides if he wants to go there. At shopping centre taxi stands, the cab drivers are more likely to go to any destination, including suburbs. (These are 1986 rates.)

You can call for a radio-taxi which will pick you up and charge an additional M$1. Call 241–4241 or 293–6211. Sometimes the lines can be very busy.

Some taxi drivers try to cheat tourists by not turning on the meter or demanding a specific amount to go a certain place. Make sure the meter is set at 70 *sen* when you get in or ask it be turned on. If the driver refuses, find another cab and report him to the Director of Road Transport, Kompleks Pejabat Damansara, Blok A, Jalan Dungun, Damansara Heights, KL.

Long Distance Taxis

Long distance taxis are hired at the Pudu Raya Terminal car parking garage. Ignore the people on the street outside who will offer you long distance taxis — at twice the rate.

Long distance taxis go to Malacca, the National Park and many other locations for about twice the bus fare. They are fast, comfortable and usually available — particularly in the morning. There is a set fare based on the destination that is divided by the four passengers. For a couple of *ringgits* more you may be able to get an air-conditioned taxi. Discuss your return trip with your driver because getting back at night is sometimes a problem.

Long distance taxis, however, are known for their bad drivers. The car accident rate in Malaysia is very high so before you get in, insist on a slow driver. You may have to wait for another cab.

Buses

Within Kuala Lumpur, there are mini-buses and larger buses which charge about 50 *sen* and are crowded. There is no written bus schedule. You can also take a large, air-conditioned first class bus to most of the major cities and to Singapore for low rates. Most buses leave from the Pudu Raya Terminal while those going to the east coast leave from Medan Tuanku off Jalan Tuanku Abdul Rahman. Buy your ticket several days in advance to get a reserved seat in the rear, which is considered the safest place.

Trishaws

There are a few trishaws left in the Chinatown area. They charge about M$1 a km. Negotiate first.

Driving

An international driving license is needed to rent a car. Daily rates are steep, between M$125–$300. Although Malaysia's roads are quite good, driving is exhausting because of the chances taken by other motorists in passing on hills and curves. Seat belts are required by law and there is a M$200 fine if you don't put them on — a law that is very effective. A driver who flashes his headlights is demanding the right-of-way — even if he is doing something illegal.

If you get in a minor accident, you are required to report to the City Traffic Police on Jalan Bandar within 24 hours. If you don't the other side may come in with a different story that puts you in the wrong. Despite this, most people "settle" the cost of the damage right on the spot. You can ask to go to a garage for an estimate or just make a deal there. A small dent is about M$50.

Communications

Telephones are available at petrol stations, many small restaurants, and on the street. Local calls are 10 *sen* but you pay extra for private phones in stores. Malaysia switched to seven digit numbers in 1985, so you may need to convert old numbers before dialing. To book an international call, dial 108. You can dial directly to Singapore and towns within Malaysia, but if the lines are busy — which is often — place the call through an operator by dialing 101. Information is 103, but is often engaged. The area code for Kuala Lumpur is 03.

At the front of the telephone directory, there is a valuable index for government offices, giving the names in English. If you are totally lost, the Government Information Department is helpful regarding government offices (298–8235 or 298–3355). The telephone directory warns you not to make calls during an electrical storm. Most residents unplug electric appliances and do not iron during storms.

Telegrams and telexes can be sent from the major hotels and from telegraph offices. The English language local papers are *The Star, The New Straits Times*, and the *Malay Mail*. Most hotel news stands carry international newspapers. There are three television channels, TV 3 being the most Westernized, and four government radio channels.

There is a lackadaisical attitude around telephones — a government line may ring for a long time and then be busy. Keep trying. Pay close attention to working hours — phones will not be answered during the long lunches or after 4:30 p.m. If the secretary barks, "What," repeat slowly, do not shout. "You hang on," is a commonly used phrase.

Electricity

Electricity is 220 volts and 50 cycles.

Language

Bahasa Malaysia is the national language, although English is widely spoken. Some common *Bahasa* words are: north — *utara*, south — *selatan*, east — *timur*, west — *barat*, street — *jalan*, one way street — *jalan sehala*, caution — *awas*, building complex — *wisma*, exit — *keluar*, enter — *masuk*, lane — *lorong*, city centre — *pusat bandaraya*, village — *kampung*, river — *sungai*, no — *tidak*, thank you — *terima kasih*, good morning — *selamat pagi*, rice — *nasi*, noodles — *mee*, fish — *ikan*, chicken — *ayam*, pig — *babi*, prawns — *udang*, coffee — *kopi*, water — *air*, drink — *minum*, eat — *makan*, how much does it cost — *berapa harga*, toilet — *tandas*, small shop — *kedai*. Two most commonly used words are "*boleh*" for can and "*tak boleh*" for cannot, substitutes for "yes" and "no." "Lah" is the Malaysian exclamation mark.

Thefts

Motorcyclists have been known to grab purses as women walk along the sidewalk, so wear your purse on the inner side. Malaysian streets are generally safer than those in most Western countries. Foreign women have found they can go to markets alone at night with no problems. But car jockeys can be a threat. Sometimes at night when you park your car downtown, a young man will demand money to wipe the window or protect it from harm — from him. If he is threatening, it is probably better to pay the 50 *sen* or M$1. Others help you back out for 20 *sen*.

Tours

Three tour companies that provide Kuala Lumpur tours are:
— Tour Fifty One Sdn. Bhd., 261–8830.
— MASMARA Travel & Tours Sdn. Bhd., 243–2333.
— Mayflower Acme Tours Sdn. Bhd., 626–7011.

The most common tours include an outer-Kuala Lumpur "country" tour, a city tour, a cultural tour that takes in Petaling Street and a Malay dinner show, a Malacca tour, a Crab Island tour, and a Templer's Park tour.

The city and country tours are probably the most helpful to get oriented. The country tour goes to a pewter centre, a *batik* factory, Batu Caves, a scorpion farm, a rubber plantation and the Kenny Hills suburb (Bukit Tunku) — all places hard to get to on your own. But some tourists have been disappointed because some guides speak poor English, know little about the destinations, and refuse to walk up to Batu Caves, let alone give much information on it.

Emergencies

Dial 999 for emergency police help or ambulance service, but a taxi may be faster.

Hours

Government office hours are Monday through Thursday 8 a.m.–12:45 p.m. and 2–4:15 p.m. Friday hours are 8 a.m.–12:15 p.m. and from 2:30–4:15 p.m. Saturday hours are from 8 a.m.–12:45 p.m. Lunch hours get extended. In five states — Johor, Kedah, Perlis, Kelantan and Trengganu — the weekend is taken on Thursday and Friday.

Shops are generally open from 9:30 a.m.–7 p.m. and department stores and supermarkets are open from 10 a.m.–10 p.m., but check individual stores.

Time Difference

Malaysia, Singapore and Hong Kong are on the same time. Australia is the same time in the west of Australia and plus three hours in the east; Japan is plus one hour; France is minus seven hours; the United Kingdom is usually minus eight hours but minus seven hours in the summer; and the United States is minus 13 hours in the east and minus 16 hours in the west.

Museums

The National Museum has quite a good cultural display showing traditional Malay crafts, customs, and games with life-size models depicting a royal wedding and circumcision of a prince. To really understand the exhibits, buy the museum's booklet called "Cultural Gallery: A Brief Guide." There are also other excellent booklets on sale — not available elsewhere — on forts, the National History Gallery, and the country's museums. The hours are from 9 a.m.–6 p.m. daily. On Fridays the museum is closed from 12–2:45 p.m. Admission is free.

The National Art Gallery has a permanent collection of almost 2,000 Malaysian artworks. Open 10 a.m.–6 p.m. daily. Friday closed from 12–12:30 p.m.

The University of Malaya has the best comprehensive collection of ceramics in Southeast Asia at its Museum of Asian Art or Muzium Seni Asia. At the University signs are in *Bahasa* Malaysia, the national language, and many buildings are not labelled, so ask at the guardhouse for directions.

Tourist Information Offices

The Tourist Development Corp. is headquartered in the Putra World Trade Centre, 24–27 floor, Menara Dato Onn (293–5188). They are open Monday through Friday from 8:30 a.m.–4:45 p.m. and on Saturday from 8:30 a.m.–1 p.m. If you have trouble reaching them by phone — their line is often busy, it is probably best to go there and collect all the schedules and brochures at once. Or go to the Visitors Centre (230–1369), which has the same hours and is located next to the National Art Gallery, across from the railway station. This centre sells Lani's Kuala Lumpur Discovery Map, the best tourist map of the city.

Toilets

Malaysia is gradually switching to Western-style toilets but there are still a number of "squat" ones around — reportedly a more natural position. Toilets rarely have toilet paper, so buy a box of small tissue packets and carry a packet with you.

Malay Customs and Taboos

Malays eat with their right hand and avoid doing anything with the left, including shaking hands or taking objects. Small restaurants have a silver tea pot on the table, containing water for washing your right hand, by itself. Rural men and women usually do not shake hands with each other, although it is common in the city. Western women should just nod hello unless a Malay man offers his hand. The handshake is not a firm grip but just a touching of fingers. The "salam" greeting consists of using both your hands in a gentle shake then touching them to your heart, meaning "a greeting from my heart."

Point with your right thumb, not your finger. It is an insult to slam your fist into an open palm. When passing in front of someone, bend over and extend your right hand. Never put your feet up on a table and point your soles at anyone — although other customs are fading in Kuala Lumpur, this one still is considered very important. Take off your shoes when entering a Malay home, and many other K.L. homes.

It is forbidden, *haram*, for Muslims to eat pork or animals that have not been killed according to religious practices. Food that is prepared in accordance with Muslim beliefs is *halal*, and you will see *halal* signs at at Kentucky Fried Chicken, McDonald's and other chain restaurants.

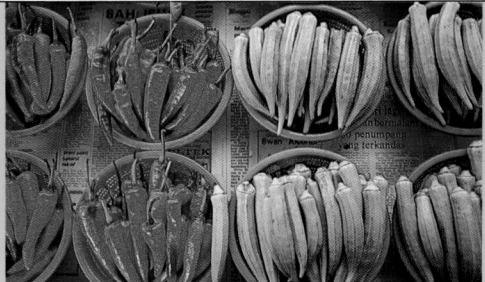

Muslims cannot touch the wet hair or saliva of a dog or allow a dog to jump up on them. Therefore, bringing pet dogs into Malaysia is problematic.

When addressing a Malay, use the first name with the polite title *Cik* for women and *Encik* for men — pronounced "chick" and "enchick." In Arabic style, Malay names are followed by "*bin*" meaning son of and "*binti*" meaning daughter of and then the father's name. So these last two words are not used when speaking to someone.

Muslims who make the pilgrimage, or *haj* to Mecca, which every Muslim is supposed to do during his/her lifetime if possible, are given the title *Haji* for men and *Hajjah* for women.

Malay women wear the traditional *baju kebaya*, a two-piece dress with a fitted top that opens at the front and forms a point below the waist, or the *baju kurong*, that is cut straight across below the waist. At the National Mosque, long dresses and scarves are provided for female tourists.

A good look on customs is *Culture Shock* by JoAnn Craig, Times Books International.

Photography

Heat and humidity damage film and cameras so leave these in air-conditioned rooms when possible. Film, particularly, should not be left in a hot car. Have the film developed as soon as possible — there is a Kodak processing plant here. If you are in Malaysia for several months, buy an air-tight box, put in some silica gel drying agent and store cameras, slides and pictures in it to avoid fungus growth. (Music tapes also are attacked and ruined by fungus.)

Always ask for a discount on film. Kodachrome must be sent to Australia and takes three weeks to process. Foto Shangri-La on Jalan Sultan Ismail and in Yow Chuan Plaza is one of the best photo stores in town. Cameras are cheaper in other countries. You can take photographs in temples, but it is polite to ask first. Only Muslims can go into a mosque at prayer times. Sometimes you can take photos from the outside looking into the prayer area but ask permission.

Foods

Popular foods include: Malay — *satay*, *nasi goreng*, *nasi lemak*, *mee rebus*, beef *rendang*, *sambal udang*, and *ikan bilis*. Indian — *nasi briyani*, *tandoori*, *roti canai*, *murtabak*, *dhal*, and banana leaf curry. Chinese — Hainanese chicken rice, *kang kong*, *mee sup*, Penang *char kway teow*, Penang *asam laksa*, *long yook* or dried meat, and *popiah* but it is hard to find in K.L. (For a more complete listing see the text and Best Bets.)

Hotels

There are a number of new first class hotels in Kuala Lumpur. Some hotels give discounts as high as 50 per cent. Most hotels charge a steep 15 per cent government and service tax on top of the prices listed. The telephone area code for Kuala Lumpur is 03.

Expensive

Equatorial Hotel, 300 rooms
Jalan Sultan Ismail, 261–2022.
K.L. Hilton Hotel, 589 rooms
Jalan Sultan Ismail, 242–2222.
Holiday Inn, 189 rooms
Jalan Pinang, 248–1066.
Ming Court Hotel, 440 rooms
Jalan Ampang, 261–8888.
Oriental Hotel, 470 rooms
Jalan Bukit Bintang.
Shangri-La Hotel, 722 rooms
11 Jalan Sultan Ismail, 232–2388.

Moderate

Hotel Malaya, 250 rooms
Jalan Hang Lekir, 232–7722.
K.L. Mandarin, 150 rooms
2–8 Jalan Sultan, 230–4533.
Fortuna Hotel, 100 rooms
87 Jalan Berangan, 241–9111.
Hotel Furama, 100 rooms
Jalan Sultan, 230–1777.
South East Asia Hotel, 208 rooms
69 Jalan Haji Hussein, 292–6077. Ask about student discounts and travel.

Cheap

Coliseum Hotel, 10 rooms
98–100 Jalan Tuanku Abdul Rahman, 292–6270
Colonial Hotel, 36 rooms
39–45 Jalan Sultan, 238–0336.
Hotel Dunia, 15 rooms
142 Jalan Petaling, 238–3978.
Hotel Sentosa, 45 rooms
316 Jalan Raja Laut, 292–5644.
Shiraz Hotel, 50 rooms
1 Jalan Medan Tuanku, 292–0159.
Tivoli Hotel, 18 rooms
136 Jalan Tuanku Abdul Rahman, 292–4108.

Hostels

Wisma Belia (274–4890), 40 Jalan Syed Putra, 110 rooms, dormitory without bath M$20, double with bath and air-con., M$35. This is a semi-government hostel a bit out of town.

YMCA (274–1439), 95 Jalan Kandang Kerbau, 60 rooms, dormitory only for men M$10. Rooms for both sexes: single without air-con., M$18, double M$25, single with air-con and bath M$40, double M$50. This hostel is in the Brickfields area, somewhat out of town.

YWCA (230–2510), 12 Jalan Hang Jebat, sleeps 15, for women only, single M$18, double M$33.

Youth Hostel (626–0872), 9 Jalan Vethavanam, 3½ mile Jalan Ipoh, sleeps 50, members M$4.50, non-members M$5.50. Also rather out of town.

Festivals and Holidays

The days for most festivals vary from year to year so only the months are given.

January – February:

Chinese New Year — *Kong Hee Fatt Choy*, a happy new year, is the regular greeting for this celebration which is marked with dragon dances and money in red packets (*ang pows*) for children.

Thaipusam — Hindu devotees honour Lord Subramaniam by carrying metal frames, called *kavadis*, up the 272 steps of Batu Caves and by piercing their cheeks with spears. The chariot procession begins at the Sri Maha Mariamman Temple, Jalan Bandar.

February 1:

Kuala Lumpur City Day — The country's capital is honoured, usually with park activities.

March – April:

Panguni Uttiram — This Hindu celebration marks the marriages of Lord Subramaniam to Theivani and of Shiva to Shakti. In Kuala Lumpur, a temple in Sentul holds a colourful procession with Lord Subramaniam on a silver chariot.

Cheng Beng — This is Chinese All Soul's Day during which Chinese clean and make offerings at the graves of relatives. In Kuala Lumpur many families go to the Old Airport Road Cemetery for a cheerful outing and do not mind explaining the procedure to foreigners who visit the cemetery.

April – May

Vesak Day — On this day Lord Buddha's birth, death and enlightenment are all celebrated. Birds are sold in bags at the temples to be let free as a gesture of releasing a captured soul. A candle-lit procession begins at the International Buddhist Pagoda in Brickfields, where there are three large statues of Buddha in the centre's Temple.

June 4

Birthday of the King (Yang di-Pertuan Agong) — Cultural activities and other festivities are held to honour the royal head of state.

June – August

Ramadan — *Muslims* cannot eat or drink from sunrise to sunset for 30 days during this fasting month, known as *Bulan Puasa* in *Bahasa* Malaysia. Elaborate Koran reading contests and cultural shows are held at Kuala Lumpur's Merdeka Stadium and are widely televised.

The end of the month is Hari Raya Puasa and two days of celebrating follow. The king, prime minister, and top government officials hold open houses where the public, including tourists, can shake hands and have a photo taken with the leaders of the country, and try Malay food. The open houses are published in the newspapers.

August

Festival of the Hungry Ghosts — On this day the souls of the dead are released from purgatories to be entertained on earth, according to Chinese beliefs. The spirits are treated to food offerings, opera and other kinds of entertainment.

August 31

National Day — Merdeka, or Independence, which occurred in 1957, is celebrated in Kuala Lumpur with a massive parade, parachute jumpers and bands. The event usually takes place on the *padang* beginning at 8 a.m. with the arrival of the king.

August – September

Hari Raya Haji — This is a national holiday in honour of the *Muslims* who made a pilgrimage, or *haj*, to Mecca and dinners are held.

September

Moon Cake Festival — This colourful festival celebrates the vanquishing of the Mongol lords in China. In Kuala Lumpur's Chinatown, the shops come alive with plastic lanterns, depicting anything from a fish to a helicopter, and special cakes, some containing a bright orange duck egg.

September – October

Festival of the Nine Emperor Gods — This Chinese nine-day festival begins with an evening procession through Kampung Ampang, on the outskirts of Kuala Lumpur and ends with a fire walking ceremony at the village's Kau Ong Yah Temple.

October – November

Deepavali — The "Way of Light" is celebrated by burning oil lamps outside Hindu homes. In Kuala Lumpur, the celebrations take place at the main temples, particularly the Sri Maha Mariamman Temple on Jalan Bandar, early in the morning. Hindu families hold open houses for family and friends.

September – December

Awal Muharram — This is the beginning of the *Muslim* year and is celebrated quietly.

November – December

Birthday of Prophet Mohammad — In Kuala Lumpur, *Muslims* gather at the National Mosque to hear the king and other leaders speak and after the services, children line up for food.

Index/Glossary

A

Abdul Rahman, Tunku (prince), 28, 29, 53, 72, 80
Abdul Razak, Tun, 29
Abdul Samad, Sultan, *26*, 26, 27, 30, 81
Abdullah, Raja, 17, 19, 26
agar agar (red seaweed jelly), 54
Alliance Party, 28, 29
amok (a crazed person), 73
antiques, 82
Architecture
  Chinese, *17*, 75, 76, 79
  Dutch, 74, 76, 77,
  European, *17*, 27, *37*, 37, 43, 74, 75, 76, 77, 79
  Indian, *16*, *55*, 75, 77
  Middle-eastern (Islamic), *cover*, *2–3*, *4–5*, 15, 27, *30*, 74
  Malay, 34, 40, 72, 76
art galleries, 83
attap (roof thatch), 16, 74

B

bahasa (See language, Malay.)
Bandar (town), 80
batik (process of dyeing fabric), *61*, *64–65*, 78, 81, 82, 87
Batu Caves, *10–11*, *48–49*, 54, 81, 83, 91
beef rendang (dry curry beef), 54
beri-beri, 27
Best Bets, 82–83
bilal (Muslim who calls devotees to prayer), 48
birdsinging contests, 59, 63, 79
bomoh (Malay medicine man), 16, 34, *53*, 53, 66
books and bookstores, 82
Brickfields community, 27, 59, 91
British, 17, 20, 28, 30, 31, 72, 73
  Non-intervention policy of, 26, 30
  residential system of, 31
  World War II role in, 34
Buddhism, 48, 53, 59, 75, 77, 80, 91
Bugis, 17, 26
Bukit Gasing (Top Spinning Hill), 80
Bukit Nanas (Pineapple Hill), 20, 79
bulat (round), 38

C

Cameron Highlands, 31, *32–33*
Capitan China, 19, 26, 30
Carey Island (Pulau Carey), 80
Central Market, 29, 77
Chartered Bank, 28, 74
chempedak (a tangy, yellow fruit), 43
Chetties (Indian money lenders), 72
Chinatown, 30, *43*, 48, *75*, 75, *76*, 76, 77, 91
Chinese, 16, 17, 26, 28, 29, 34, 40, 43, 51, 53, 72, 73, 74, 75, 76, 78, 81
  early miners, 16, 19, 26
  funerals for, 59, *58–59*
  mansions of, 79
  mining companies, 28, 30
  riots of, 27–28
Chong Yun Long opera, *56–57*
Church of St. Mary the Virgin, 74
City Hall, 74, 82

civil war (See Selangor Civil War.)
Clarke, Sir Andrew, 26
coffee, 27, 31
Coliseum Cafe, 74, 79, 83
Commercial Press, 76
communists, 28, 40, 73
Confrontation, 29
Coq d'Or, Le. 72, 79, 83
Crab Island (Pulau Ketam), *42*, 81, *84–85*
crafts, 82
curry tiffin (a Sunday curry lunch), 37
customs and entry rules, 86

D

dadah (drugs), 45, 53, 86
dakwahs (conservative Muslims), 51
datuk or dato (honorary title for non-royal males), 78
Davidson, James Guthrie, 26, 30
Dayabumi Complex, *cover*, 74, 82
dim sum (Chinese tidbits or snacks), 75, 83
discos, 82
Douglas, Captain Bloomfield, 26, 30
dressmaker and hairstyling, 82
durian (a strong, creamy fruit), 45, 72
Dutch, 17, 20, 79, 81

E

Emergency, 28, 40, 73

F

Federal Council, 27
Federated Malay States, 27, 31, 72
Federation of Malaya, 28
festivals and holidays, 91
floods, 27, 28, *29*, 30
Forest Research Institute, 80
Fraser's Hill, 31
Friends of the Heritage of Malaysia Society, 37

G

gasing (top spinning), 63
Gedung Raja Abdullah Museum, 80
General Post Office, former and present, 74
Gent, Sir Edward, *40*
Genting Highlands, 80, 81
Guinness Brewery, 79

H

haj (Muslim pilgrimage to Mecca), *Haji* (man's title), *Hajjah* (woman's title), 90, 91
halal (prepared in accordance with Muslim beliefs), 89
hantu (ghost), 53
haram (against Muslim beliefs), 89
Hari Raya, 54, 64
Hash House Harriers, 72
health and hospitals, 86–87
Heritage of Malaysia Trust, 29
High Court Building, *2–3*, 74
Hinduism, 48, *48–49*, 53, 54, 66, 91
Historical Chronology, 26–29
hotels, 90

I

ice kacang (snow-cone with beans), 43, 77
ikan bilis (dried fish), 43
imam (presiding elder in a mosque), 54
Independence (Merdeka), 28, 34, 37, 40, 72, 91
India, 15, 28, 31, 78
Indians, 15, 16, 20–21, 28, 34, 43, 45, 51, 53, 72, 75, 77, 78
  dress of, 54
  Tamil workers, 31, 73
Indonesia, 17, 29, 59, *62–63*, 66, 79, 86
Industrial Court Building (formerly Chow Kit Emporium), 74
Information Department, 40, *74*, 74, 88
Institute of Medical Research, 27
International Crafts Museum, 78
Islam, 40, 48, 53, 66, 81
istana (palace), 81

J

jalan (street), used throughout text.
Janda Baik, 80

K

kampung (village), 34, 38, 64, 76
Kampung Ampang, 59, 79, 91
Kampung Baru (New Village), 34, *39*, 67, 81
Kampung Datuk Keramat, 79
Kampung Sungei Penchala, 81, 82
Karyaneka Handicraft Centre, 78, 82
kavadi (large metal frame), 54, 91
kebaya labuh (a traditional Malay, long-sleeved dress), *39*
kedai kopi (coffe shop), 43
Kelantan and Trengganu, *60*, 63, 78, 89
Kenny Hills (Bukit Tunku), 80
keramat (holy tomb or place), 79
ketayap (Muslim prayer cap), 67
ketupat (compressed, cold rice), 43
King, 28, 29, 73, 91
Kingfisher Head Kris, *66*, 66
kite flying, *60*, 63
K.L. Trivia, 72–73
Klang (also spelled Kelang), 19, 27, 28, 30, 31, 80, 81
Klang and Gombak rivers, *2–3*, *14*, 16, 17, 19, 26, 27, 28, *29*, 29, 30, 73, *74*, 74, *76*, *78*
Koran (also spelled Quran), 16, 43, 53, 64, 78, 91
kris (wavy dagger), 63, 64, *66*, 66, 78
Kuala Selangor, 81
Kudin, Tunku (prince), 19, 26
Kutang Kraft, *61*, 81, 82
kwai lo (foreign devil), 73

L

Lake Club, 31
Lake Gardens (Taman Tasek Perdana), 27, 31, 81
language, Malay *(bahasa)*, 28, 73, 88, 91
Lat (Mohammad Nor Khalid), *38*, 38
lebuhraya (highway), *15*
Loke Chow Kit, 74, 77, 79

Loke Hall (PAM building), 74, 79
Loke Yew, 79

M

Mahdi, Raja (prince), 17, 19, 20
Majestic Hotel, 29, *37*, 37, 89
Malacca, 17, 19, 20, 26, 38, 73, 86, 87
malaria, 16, 28, 34, 87
Malayan Chinese Association (MCA), 28, 29, 37
Malayan Communist Party, 28
Malayan Indian Congress (MIC), 28, 37
Malayan People's Anti-Japanese Army (MPAJA), 28
Malay Union, 28
Malays, 15, 16, 17, 19, 28, 29, 30, 34, 38, 40, 43, 53, 77, 78, 81
  agricultural settlement, 31, 34
  customs of, 89
  political power, 28, 29
  UMNO, 28
Maps
  Around the Padang Walking Tour, 74
  Central Kuala Lumpur, 71
  Chinatown Architectural Tour, 76
  Chinatown Cultural Tour, 75
  Chow Kit Market, 77
  Kuala Lumpur and Environs, 70
  Malaysia in the Region, 70
  Shopping Tour, 78
Markets
  Chow Kit Market, 43, *44–45*, 77, 77, 81
  Kampung Baru Sunday (on Saturday) Market, 81
  Kampung Datuk Keramat, 79
  Petaling Street Market, *18–19*, 66, 75, 79, 81
  Pudu Market, 77, 81
  Tuanku Abdul Rahman Market, 81
Market Square, old (now Medan Pasar), 20, *24–25*, 30, 74, 76, 77
Masjid (mosque) Jame, 16, 34, *74*, 74, 77, *94–95*
Masjid Jamek Pakistan, 77
Masjid Negara (See National Mosque.)
Masjid Sultan Salahuddin, 72
mat salleh (white person), 73
Maugham, Somerset, 72, 74
mee hoon sup (rice vermicelli soup), 43
merbuk (a singing bird), 59
Merdeka (See Independence.)
money, tipping and bargaining, 87
Muhammad, Sultan, 17, 19
Muslims, *6–7*, 15, *20–21*, *41*, 43, 48, *51*, 51, 53, 64, *67*, 72, 74, 77, 86, 87, 90, 91
Muzium Negara (See National Museum.)
Muzium Seni Asia (Museum of Asian Art), 80, 89

N

National Art Gallery (Balai Seni Lukis Negara), 29, *37*, 37, 40, 89

National Front coalition, 28
National Mosque (Masjid Negara), *6–7*, *41*, *51*, 51, 54, 90, 91
National Museum (Muzium Negara), 34, 40, 73, 80, 89
New Economic Policy (NEP), 29
New Islamic Centre Complex, *4–5*
Nine Emperor Gods festival, *8–9*, 59, 91
Norman, A.C., 74

O

Off the Beaten Track, 79–81
Old Airport Road Cemetery, 80, 91
opium, 19, 27, 30, 31, 79
Orang Asli, 80, 81
orang minyak (oily man), 73
orang putih (white person), 73
orchids, 80

P

padang (field), 28, 34, *74*, *74*, 91
palm oil, 15, 73
Pan Pacific Hotel and Putra World Trade Centre, 72, 89
parang (large knife), 79
Penang, 17, 19, 31
petai beans (a long green bean), 77
population, 15, 17, 86
Port Klang (also spelled Kelang), 80, 81
Public Works Department, 74
Pudu Prison, 72

R

Railway Station, K.L., *30*, 31, 34, 37
Ramadan, 54, 91
restaurants, 83
Ridley, H.N., 31
roti canai (thrown bread), 45, 78
roti man, *20*
rubber, 15, 27, 31

S

Sabah and Sarawak, 17, 29, 66, 78, 86
Sallehuddin, Sultan, 26
Sanitary Board, 27, 74
sari (wrap-around Indian dress), 54, 78
sarong (Malay skirt or cradle), 45, 51, 73, 78
satay (barbequed spicy meat), 43, 45
Secretariat (See Sultan Abdul Samad Building.)
Chinese Assembly Hall,
Selangor, 76
Selangor Civil War, 17, 19, 26, 30, 79, 80
Selangor Club, 31, *34*, 34, 72, 74, 81
Selangor Pewter, *64*, 72, 78, 82
Selangor State, 17, 26, 27, 29, 30, 31, 80
sepak takraw (a volley-ball type game), 63
shadow play (See *wayang kulit*.)
Sheppard, Tan Sri Dato Mubin, 40, 40, 82
shopping centres, 82
Sikhs, 15, 77
songket (gold or silver woven cloth), 78
songkok (black Muslim cap), 51, 78
Stock Exchange, *35*
Straits Settlements, 17, 19

Subramaniam, Lord, *48–49*, 54, 91
Sulaiman, Raja (later sultan), *26–27*, 81
Sultan Abdul Samad Building (formerly Selangor State Secretariat), 27, 34, 74
sultans and chiefs, 17, 19, 26, 27, 28, 30, 31, 72, 73
Sungai Buloh leprosarium (National Leprosy Control Centre), *31*, 81
Supreme Court Building, 74
Swettenham, Sir Frank, 27, 30, 31, 76, 82

T

Tauchang Riots, 28
Temples, Chinese
  Chan See Shu Yuen, 76
  Chetawan, 80
  Chin Foot Sze, 80
  Hoeh Beng, 77
  International Buddhist Pagoda centre, 59, 91
  Kau Ong Yah, *8–9*, 59, 91
  Khoon Yam, 76, 80
  Kong Hock Teng, 77
  Sun Hoon Keong, *56–57*,
  Sze Ya, 75, *75*, 77
  Tham Kong, 79
  Thean Hou, 80
Temples, Indian
  Sivan, 80
  Sri Maha Mariamman, *55*, *75*, 75, 91
  Sri Subramania Swamy, *10–11*
  Tatt Khalsa Diwan, 77
Thaipusam, *10–11*, *54*, 54, 91
tin, 17, 19, 20, 26, 28, 30, 64, 80
  discovery of, 16, 26
  largest producer of, 15, 27
  legends about, 73
tofu (soybean curd), 77, 79
top spinning (*gasing*), 63
tour bus companies, 88
Tourist Development Corp., 86, 89
Tours around K.L., 74–78
Travel Notes, 86–91

U

United Malays National Organization (UMNO), 28, 37
University of Malaya, 80, 89

V

Van Hagen, 20
Venning, Alfred, 27
Vesak Day, 59, 91
Victoria Institution, 72, 75

W

wau burung (bird kite), *60*
wayang kulit (shadow play), 63
weather, 86
Wisma Loke, 79
World War II, 28, 34, 37, 40, 74, 79

Y

Yang di-Pertuan Agong (King's title), 73
Yap Ah Loy, 19, 20, 26, *28*, 30, 75

Acknowledgements

The author would like to thank the following for their contributions: The Malaysian Culture Group for assistance with tour information; The Muzium Negara Malaysia for archival photographs on pages 24–25, 26, 28 and 29 and for permitting the photographing of its collection as seen on the endpapers and page 60; The Arkib Negara Malaysia for archival photographs; The Tourist Development Corp. of Malaysia for travel information on historical buildings; Tan Sri Dato Mubin Sheppard for use of the photograph on page 40; Victor Chin of Rupa Design for permission to reprint three of his drawings on pages 74–75; Lat for the self-portrait on page 38. Other individuals who generously gave of their time and knowledge include Waveney Jenkins, Datin Margaret Ariffin, Professor Khoo Kay Kim, Hajeedar Haji Abdul Majid, Tan Sri Dato Mubin Sheppard, Sabariah Mohamed Nasiruddin, John Berthelsen, Martin Dickie, Edda de Silva, Susan Luchs, Walter Cheah, Tan Siok Choo, Lorraine Downey and many others.

Tukang Jahit Soon Kee (left) rents and sells Western and Asian wedding clothes. As in other shophouse stores, the workers eat lunch over the counter.